Understanding M the
 [

Shaping Perspectives and Identities

By
Robert M. Parker

DISCLAIMER

Copyright @ By Robert M. Parker 2023. All rights reserved.

Introduction

The process of distributing and exchanging information to sizable population segments via mass media is known as mass communication. It makes use of a variety of media because technology has improved the efficiency of information distribution. Journalism and advertising are two of the most common examples of platforms that are used and studied. In contrast to interpersonal and organizational communication, mass communication is concentrated on specific resources that disseminate information to a large number of recipients. The main focus of the study of mass communication is how the information and content that is disseminated widely influences or persuades the recipients of the information in terms of their behavior, attitude, opinion, or emotion.

Mass communication, narrowly defined, is the dissemination of messages to numerous recipients simultaneously. Mass communication, however, can be broadly defined as the practice of widely disseminating information both domestically and internationally.

Information can be swiftly spread through mass communication to a large number of people who may not even reside near the source. A variety of platforms, referred to as "mediums," are used in mass communication, including billboards, radio, television, social media, newspapers, magazines, books, movies, and the Internet. Mass communication is utilized in the modern period to quickly spread information, frequently on political and other divisive subjects.

There are strong links between our culture and the media that are ingested through mass communication, which fuels polarization and divides people along important topics.

Chapter 1

Media Studies

Media studies is an interdisciplinary field that explores how media, communication, and technology intersect with society. It encompasses a broad range of topics, from the analysis of media content and its effects on audiences to the examination of media industries, technologies, and cultural contexts. Here are key components within the field of media studies:

1. **Media Analysis:**
   - **Content Analysis:** Examining media content to identify patterns, themes, and messages.
   - **Textual Analysis:** Analyzing the structure and meaning of media texts, including written, visual, and audio content.
2. **Media Effects:**
   - **Cultural Effects:** Studying how media shapes cultural norms, values, and identities.
   - **Political Effects:** Investigating the role of media in shaping political opinions and behaviors.
   - **Psychological Effects:** Exploring the impact of media on individual attitudes, beliefs, and behaviors.
3. **Media and Society:**
   - **Media and Democracy:** Examining the role of media in democratic societies, including issues of media ownership and political communication.
   - **Media and Social Change:** Analyzing how media influences and reflects social change and activism.
4. **Media Industries:**
   - **Media Economics:** Investigating the economic

structures and business models of media industries.
- **Media Ownership:** Analyzing patterns of ownership and concentration of media outlets.

5. **Media Technologies:**
   - **Digital Media:** Studying the impact of digital technologies on media production, distribution, and consumption.
   - **Media Convergence:** Exploring the merging of traditional media forms with digital technologies.

6. **Media and Culture:**
   - **Cultural Studies:** Examining the relationships between media, culture, and power.
   - **Representation:** Analyzing how various social groups are portrayed in media and the implications of these representations.

7. **Media Literacy:**
   - **Critical Media Literacy:** Teaching individuals to critically analyze and interpret media messages.
   - **Media Education:** Promoting skills and knowledge for navigating a media-saturated environment.

8. **Media History:**
   - **Historical Analysis:** Studying the historical development of media technologies, institutions, and practices.

9. **Global Media:**
   - **International Communication:** Examining the global flow of media content and the impact of media on a global scale.
   - **Media Imperialism:** Analyzing power dynamics in international media relations.

10. **Research Methods in Media Studies:**

- **Qualitative and Quantitative Methods:** Employing various research methodologies to study media phenomena.
- **Surveys, Interviews, and Content Analysis:** Common research techniques used in media studies.

Media studies is a dynamic and evolving field, constantly adapting to changes in technology, society, and media practices. It encourages critical thinking and a deeper understanding of the role media plays in shaping our world.

Media History

Media history is a fascinating field that examines the development and evolution of various communication technologies and forms of media over time. It encompasses the evolution of communication from ancient times to the present day. Here are some key aspects and periods in media history:

1. **Oral Tradition:**
    - The earliest form of communication relied on oral traditions, where stories, knowledge, and information were passed down verbally from generation to generation.
2. **Written Communication:**
    - The invention of writing systems marked a significant shift, allowing information to be recorded and transmitted through written texts. This period includes ancient civilizations like Mesopotamia, Egypt, and China.
3. **Printing Press and Early Print Media (15th Century):**
    - Johannes Gutenberg's invention of the printing press around 1440 revolutionized mass communication by making books, newspapers, and pamphlets more widely accessible. This marked the beginning of the print media era.
4. **Newspapers and Periodicals (17th-18th Centuries):**
    - The rise of newspapers and periodicals in the 17th and 18th centuries played a crucial role in disseminating news, information, and opinions. This period saw the emergence of a more structured and organized press.
5. **Telegraph and Telecommunications (19th Century):**

- The invention of the telegraph in the 19th century significantly improved long-distance communication. It played a key role in news reporting and connecting people across large distances.

6. **Radio Broadcasting (20th Century):**
   - The development of radio broadcasting in the early 20th century revolutionized the way information and entertainment were delivered. It became a powerful medium for news, music, and storytelling.

7. **Television (Mid-20th Century):**
   - The introduction of television in the mid-20th century brought visual storytelling into homes around the world. It became a dominant medium for news, entertainment, and advertising.

8. **Internet and Digital Media (Late 20th Century - Present):**
   - The advent of the internet and digital technologies has transformed the media landscape. It has led to the rise of online journalism, social media, streaming services, and other digital platforms.

9. **Social Media (21st Century):**
   - The proliferation of social media platforms in the 21st century has changed the dynamics of communication, enabling individuals to share information and interact on a global scale.

10. **Emerging Technologies (Present and Future):**
    - Ongoing developments in technology, including virtual reality, augmented reality, and artificial intelligence, continue to shape the future of media and communication.

Studying media history provides valuable insights into how communication technologies have influenced societies, shaped cultures, and impacted the way information is disseminated and consumed.

Media Effects

Media effects refer to the impact that media content, technologies, and platforms have on individuals, society, and culture. Researchers in media studies and related fields explore various dimensions of media effects to understand how media influences attitudes, behaviors, and perceptions. There are several categories of media effects, and research often focuses on both short-term and long-term consequences. Here are some key types of media effects:

1. **Cognitive Effects:**
   - **Knowledge and Information:** Media can influence what individuals know and believe by presenting information, news, and educational content.
   - **Agenda-setting:** The media's ability to shape the public's perception of issues by highlighting certain topics and downplaying others.
2. **Attitudinal Effects:**
   - **Attitude Change:** Media can contribute to changes in attitudes and opinions by presenting persuasive messages and framing issues in particular ways.
   - **Attitude Reinforcement:** Media can reinforce existing attitudes by providing content that aligns with viewers' preexisting beliefs.
3. **Behavioral Effects:**
   - **Imitation and Modeling:** Media, especially in the form of entertainment, can influence behavior by providing role models and shaping social norms.
   - **Violence and Aggression:** Research has explored the potential link between exposure to violent

media content and aggressive behavior.
4. **Emotional Effects:**
    - **Emotional Responses:** Media can evoke emotional reactions, such as joy, fear, sadness, or anger, influencing the audience's emotional state.
    - **Desensitization:** Prolonged exposure to certain types of media content may lead to reduced emotional responsiveness over time.
5. **Social Effects:**
    - **Socialization:** Media plays a role in socializing individuals by conveying cultural norms, values, and expectations.
    - **Social Influence:** Media can shape social norms and influence behavior by presenting certain behaviors as acceptable or desirable.
6. **Political Effects:**
    - **Political Socialization:** Media contributes to the formation of political beliefs and attitudes, particularly in terms of civic engagement and political participation.
    - **Agenda-Setting in Politics:** Media can influence public opinion by determining which political issues receive attention.
7. **Health Effects:**
    - **Body Image and Self-Esteem:** Media, especially in the context of advertising and entertainment, can impact individuals' perceptions of beauty and self-worth.
    - **Health Behavior:** Media can influence health-related behaviors, such as diet, exercise, and

substance use.
8. **Cultural Effects:**
    - **Cultural Identity:** Media contributes to the construction and reinforcement of cultural identities, including ethnicity, gender, and nationality.
    - **Cultural Globalization:** Media influences the global spread of cultural elements, leading to cultural convergence or hybridization.

It's important to note that the relationship between media and its effects is complex, and researchers often consider individual differences, contextual factors, and the interactive nature of media consumption. Additionally, media effects can be positive, negative, or neutral, depending on the content and context. The study of media effects contributes to our understanding of the role media plays in shaping society and individuals.

Media Ethics

Media ethics refers to the principles, standards, and guidelines that guide the behavior of professionals in the media industry. It involves considerations of moral values, responsibility, and the impact of media practices on individuals and society. Ethical decision-making in media is crucial to maintaining public trust, ensuring accuracy, and upholding the integrity of journalism and other forms of communication. Here are key areas and principles within media ethics:

1. **Accuracy and Truthfulness:**
    - **Verification:** Media professionals have a responsibility to verify information before publishing or broadcasting it to ensure accuracy.
    - **Correction of Errors:** If errors are identified, media organizations should promptly correct them and provide accurate information to the audience.
2. **Fairness and Objectivity:**
    - **Fair Reporting:** Media should present a balanced and impartial view of events, providing multiple perspectives and avoiding bias.
    - **Avoiding Conflicts of Interest:** Journalists and media organizations should disclose and minimize conflicts of interest that could compromise their objectivity.
3. **Independence:**
    - **Editorial Independence:** Media outlets should resist undue influence from advertisers, government entities, or other external sources that could compromise journalistic integrity.

- **Avoiding Political Bias:** Journalists should strive to separate news reporting from personal political views and affiliations.

4. **Privacy:**
   - **Respecting Privacy:** Media professionals should respect individuals' privacy rights and avoid intrusion into private matters without a compelling public interest.
   - **Informed Consent:** Obtaining informed consent when reporting on personal or sensitive issues is an ethical consideration.

5. **Sensitivity and Diversity:**
   - **Avoiding Harm:** Media should be mindful of the potential harm that could result from their reporting, especially in sensitive situations or when dealing with vulnerable populations.
   - **Diversity and Representation:** Media organizations should strive to represent diverse voices and perspectives, avoiding stereotypes and promoting inclusivity.

6. **Accountability:**
   - **Accountability for Mistakes:** Media professionals and organizations should take responsibility for their mistakes, openly acknowledge them, and take steps to prevent recurrence.
   - **Transparency:** Being transparent about the sources, methods, and motivations behind media content helps build trust with the audience.

7. **Public Interest:**
   - **Serving the Public Interest:** Media should

prioritize the public interest, providing information that is valuable to the audience and contributing to an informed citizenry.
- **Resisting Sensationalism:** Avoid sensationalism and clickbait journalism that prioritizes attention-grabbing headlines over substance.

8. **Social Media Ethics:**
   - **Verification of Social Media Content:** Media professionals should verify information sourced from social media before reporting it.
   - **Engaging Responsibly:** Responsible and ethical use of social media platforms, avoiding the spread of misinformation or participating in online harassment.

9. **Protection of Sources:**
   - **Confidentiality:** Journalists should protect the identity of confidential sources to encourage open communication and the exposure of important information.

10. **Media Ownership and Control:**
    - **Avoiding Monopoly and Bias:** Media organizations should strive for diverse ownership and avoid monopolistic control to prevent bias and ensure pluralism.

Media ethics is a dynamic field that evolves alongside changes in technology, society, and media practices. Professionals in the media industry must continually reflect on ethical considerations to maintain public trust and uphold the principles of responsible journalism and communication.

Media Literacy

Media literacy refers to the ability to access, analyze, evaluate, and create media content critically. It involves a set of skills and competencies that enable individuals to navigate the complex media landscape, understand the messages conveyed, and make informed decisions about the information they encounter. Media literacy is crucial in the modern world, where people are constantly exposed to a variety of media sources. Here are the key components of media literacy:

1. **Access:**
   - **Understanding Media Landscape:** Recognizing different media platforms, including traditional and digital sources.
   - **Accessing Information:** Knowing how to find and access media content through various channels.
2. **Analysis:**
   - **Critical Thinking:** Developing the ability to question and analyze media messages critically.
   - **Media Messages and Techniques:** Understanding how media messages are constructed, including the use of language, visuals, and sound.
3. **Evaluation:**
   - **Assessing Credibility:** Determining the reliability and credibility of media sources.
   - **Bias Recognition:** Identifying potential biases in media content and understanding the influence of perspectives and agendas.
4. **Creation:**
   - **Media Production Skills:** Developing the ability to

create media content, including writing, visual design, and digital production.
- **Understanding Media Influence:** Recognizing the impact of media production on shaping public opinions and attitudes.

5. **Ethical Considerations:**
   - **Understanding Media Ethics:** Grasping the ethical principles and values that guide media professionals.
   - **Recognizing Manipulation:** Identifying manipulative tactics and practices in media content.

6. **Media Literacy in the Digital Age:**
   - **Digital Literacy:** Navigating digital platforms, understanding algorithms, and recognizing online privacy issues.
   - **Social Media Literacy:** Understanding the dynamics of social media, including the spread of misinformation and the influence of social networks.

7. **Cultural and Social Context:**
   - **Understanding Cultural Context:** Recognizing how media messages are shaped by cultural, social, and historical contexts.
   - **Media and Identity:** Exploring how media representations contribute to the construction of individual and collective identities.

8. **Media Literacy in Education:**
   - **Curriculum Integration:** Integrating media literacy into educational curricula to equip students with critical thinking skills.
   - **Media Literacy Programs:** Implementing programs

that promote media literacy skills from an early age.

9. **Media Literacy Advocacy:**
   - **Promoting Awareness:** Advocating for the importance of media literacy in society and promoting awareness about its benefits.
   - **Media Literacy Campaigns:** Engaging in campaigns that emphasize the need for media literacy education.

10. **Continual Learning:**
    - **Adaptability:** Recognizing that media technologies and platforms evolve, and staying updated on new developments.
    - **Lifelong Learning:** Emphasizing the importance of ongoing learning to navigate changes in the media landscape.

Media literacy empowers individuals to be discerning consumers and responsible creators of media content. It plays a crucial role in fostering an informed and engaged citizenry in a world where media plays a significant role in shaping public opinion and influencing societal norms.

Chapter 2

Journalism

Journalism is the practice of collecting, verifying, and presenting news and information to an audience. Journalists play a crucial role in providing the public with timely, accurate, and relevant information about events, issues, and developments. Journalism exists in various forms, including print, broadcast, online, and multimedia platforms. Here are the key aspects and principles of journalism:

1. **News Gathering:**
    - **Reporting:** Journalists collect information through interviews, observations, research, and other means.
    - **Sources:** Establishing and cultivating reliable sources for accurate and timely information.
2. **Writing and Editing:**
    - **News Writing:** Presenting information in a clear, concise, and engaging manner.
    - **Editing:** Ensuring accuracy, clarity, and adherence to editorial standards.
3. **Objectivity and Fairness:**
    - **Objectivity:** Striving to present facts without bias and personal opinions.
    - **Fairness:** Providing balanced coverage by representing multiple perspectives on a given issue.
4. **Ethical Considerations:**
    - **Accuracy:** Verifying information before publication to ensure accuracy.
    - **Integrity:** Upholding ethical standards, avoiding conflicts of interest, and maintaining independence.
    - **Privacy:** Respecting individuals' right to privacy

while reporting on public issues.

5. **News Values:**
   - **Timeliness:** Reporting news promptly to keep the audience informed.
   - **Relevance:** Focusing on topics that are significant to the audience.
   - **Impact:** Emphasizing the consequences and implications of events and issues.
   - **Proximity:** Prioritizing news that is geographically or emotionally close to the audience.

6. **Investigative Journalism:**
   - **In-Depth Reporting:** Conducting in-depth research and analysis to uncover hidden truths or expose wrongdoing.
   - **Public Accountability:** Holding individuals, organizations, and institutions accountable through investigative reporting.

7. **Interviewing Skills:**
   - **Conducting Interviews:** Skillfully interviewing sources to gather information and perspectives.
   - **Questioning Techniques:** Asking probing and relevant questions to elicit meaningful responses.

8. **Media Ethics:**
   - **Responsible Reporting:** Ensuring that the public interest is served without causing unnecessary harm.
   - **Disclosure:** Clearly stating any conflicts of interest and being transparent about sources.

9. **Media Law:**
   - **Libel and Defamation:** Understanding and avoiding legal issues related to false and damaging

statements.
- **Freedom of the Press:** Upholding the principles of a free press while respecting legal boundaries.

10. **Multimedia Journalism:**
    - **Digital Platforms:** Adapting to the use of digital tools and platforms for reporting, editing, and audience engagement.
    - **Visual Storytelling:** Incorporating multimedia elements such as images, videos, and infographics.

11. **Newsroom Collaboration:**
    - **Collaborative Journalism:** Working with colleagues, editors, and other professionals to enhance the quality of news coverage.
    - **Teamwork:** Collaborating with other journalists on large-scale projects or breaking news events.

12. **Adaptability and Technological Skills:**
    - **Digital Literacy:** Staying current with digital technologies, social media, and online publishing platforms.
    - **Adapting to Changes:** Embracing technological advancements and adapting reporting methods to the evolving media landscape.

Journalism serves as a cornerstone of democratic societies, providing citizens with the information they need to make informed decisions and participate in civic life. In an era of rapid technological change, journalists must navigate new challenges while upholding the core principles of accuracy, fairness, and ethical reporting.

News Reporting

News reporting is a fundamental aspect of journalism that involves gathering, verifying, and presenting information about current events, issues, and developments to the public. News reporters, also known as journalists, play a crucial role in providing timely, accurate, and relevant news coverage. Here are key elements and principles of news reporting:

1. **News Values:**
    - **Timeliness:** Reporting news promptly to keep the audience informed about recent events.
    - **Relevance:** Focusing on topics that are significant to the audience.
    - **Impact:** Emphasizing the consequences and implications of events and issues.
    - **Proximity:** Prioritizing news that is geographically or emotionally close to the audience.
2. **News Gathering:**
    - **Research:** Conducting thorough research to understand the background and context of a news story.
    - **Interviews:** Speaking with relevant sources, experts, eyewitnesses, and officials to gather information and perspectives.
    - **Observation:** Directly observing events and situations to provide firsthand accounts.
3. **Objectivity and Fairness:**
    - **Objectivity:** Striving to present facts without bias and personal opinions.
    - **Fairness:** Providing balanced coverage by

representing multiple perspectives on a given issue.
4. **Accuracy and Verification:**
    - **Verification:** Ensuring the accuracy of information by cross-referencing multiple sources and checking facts.
    - **Attribution:** Attributing information to its source and specifying when information cannot be independently verified.
5. **News Writing:**
    - **Inverted Pyramid Style:** Presenting the most important information at the beginning of the story, followed by details in descending order of importance.
    - **Clarity and Conciseness:** Writing clearly and concisely to effectively convey information.
    - **Headlines and Leads:** Crafting compelling headlines and leads to grab the audience's attention.
6. **News Story Structure:**
    - **Five W's and H:** Addressing the who, what, when, where, why, and how questions to provide comprehensive coverage.
    - **Nut Graph:** Summarizing the main point of the story and its significance.
7. **Breaking News Coverage:**
    - **Urgency:** Delivering breaking news quickly and accurately.
    - **Continuous Updates:** Providing ongoing coverage and updates as new information becomes available.
8. **Interviewing Skills:**
    - **Effective Questioning:** Asking clear, relevant, and

probing questions to gather meaningful information.
- **Active Listening:** Paying close attention to responses and adapting follow-up questions based on interviewee answers.

9. **Ethical Considerations:**
    - **Privacy:** Respecting individuals' right to privacy while reporting on public issues.
    - **Sensitivity:** Approaching sensitive topics with empathy and considering potential harm that may result from coverage.

10. **Media Technology and Tools:**
    - **Digital Tools:** Using digital tools for research, data analysis, and communication.
    - **Mobile Journalism (MoJo):** Utilizing mobile devices for on-the-spot reporting, including photo and video capture.

11. **Legal Awareness:**
    - **Libel and Defamation:** Understanding and avoiding legal issues related to false and damaging statements.
    - **Freedom of Information:** Navigating laws related to access to information and government transparency.

12. **Collaboration and Teamwork:**
    - **Newsroom Collaboration:** Working with colleagues, editors, and other professionals to enhance the quality of news coverage.
    - **Team Reporting:** Collaborating with other journalists on large-scale projects or breaking news

events.

Effective news reporting requires a combination of skills, ethical considerations, and an understanding of the principles that guide journalism. Reporters play a critical role in informing the public and contributing to an informed and engaged citizenry.

Feature Writing

Feature writing is a form of journalism that goes beyond the basic who, what, when, where, and why of news reporting. Instead, it focuses on providing in-depth, human-centered stories that engage readers on a more personal and emotional level. Feature articles often explore the background, context, and human elements of a story, offering readers a richer and more immersive experience. Here are key elements and considerations in feature writing:

1. **Human Interest:**
     - **Personal Stories:** Feature articles often center around individuals and their experiences, making the story relatable and engaging.
     - **Emotion and Empathy:** Evoking emotions and empathy by capturing the human aspects of a story.
2. **Storytelling Techniques:**
     - **Narrative Structure:** Using a narrative or storytelling structure to draw readers into the story.
     - **Descriptive Language:** Employing vivid and descriptive language to create a sensory experience for the reader.
3. **In-Depth Research:**
     - **Background Information:** Providing context and background to enhance the reader's understanding.
     - **Expert Interviews:** Consulting experts, insiders, or authorities to add depth and credibility to the story.
4. **Creativity and Style:**
     - **Feature Leads:** Crafting creative and attention-grabbing leads or introductions to captivate readers

from the beginning.
- **Writing Style:** Adopting a unique and engaging writing style that reflects the tone and theme of the feature.

5. **Theme and Angle:**
   - **Identifying Themes:** Focusing on specific themes or topics that resonate with the audience.
   - **Unique Angles:** Presenting a unique angle or perspective to distinguish the feature from standard news reporting.

6. **Structure:**
   - **Feature Structure:** Organizing the feature with a well-defined structure, including a lead, body, and conclusion.
   - **Use of Anecdotes:** Incorporating anecdotes, quotes, and examples to illustrate key points.

7. **Visual Elements:**
   - **Photography and Graphics:** Including relevant visual elements, such as photographs, infographics, or illustrations, to enhance the storytelling.
   - **Layout Considerations:** Collaborating with designers for an appealing and reader-friendly layout.

8. **Human Connection:**
   - **Creating Connection:** Building a connection between the subject of the feature and the reader.
   - **Readership Engagement:** Encouraging reader engagement through comments, discussions, or feedback.

9. **Research and Fact-Checking:**

- **Thorough Research:** Conducting thorough research to ensure accuracy and credibility.
- **Fact-checking:** Verifying all information to maintain the trust of the readers.

10. **Diverse Perspectives:**
    - **Inclusion of Voices:** Including diverse perspectives and voices to provide a well-rounded view of the topic.
    - **Representing Communities:** Ensuring fair representation of different communities and groups.
11. **Long-Form Journalism:**
    - **Extended Format:** Embracing longer formats that allow for more in-depth exploration and storytelling.
    - **Series and Instalments:** Breaking down a complex story into a series or installments for a more comprehensive approach.
12. **Impactful Endings:**
    - **Conclusion:** Crafting a memorable and impactful conclusion that leaves a lasting impression on the reader.
    - **Call to Action:** Encouraging readers to reflect, act, or further explore the topic.

Feature writing provides an opportunity to delve deeply into subjects, bringing stories to life through vivid descriptions and compelling narratives. It allows journalists to connect with readers on a personal level and explore the human experiences that lie behind the headlines.

Investigative Journalism

Investigative journalism is a form of journalism that involves in-depth research and reporting to uncover hidden truths, expose wrongdoing, and hold individuals, organizations, or institutions accountable. Investigative journalists often delve into complex and challenging topics, relying on extensive research, interviews, and analysis to bring important issues to light. Here are key aspects and considerations in investigative journalism:

1. **Deep Research:**
    - **Thorough Investigation:** Conducting in-depth research to uncover facts, patterns, and connections.
    - **Access to Documents:** Utilizing public records, government documents, and other sources to gather information.
2. **Confidential Sources:**
    - **Protection of Sources:** Safeguarding the identities of confidential sources to encourage whistleblowers and insiders to come forward.
    - **Anonymous Tips:** Investigating leads and tips received from anonymous sources.
3. **Persistence and Tenacity:**
    - **Commitment to the Story:** Pursuing a story with determination, often over an extended period.
    - **Overcoming Obstacles:** Facing challenges and obstacles, such as legal barriers or threats, with resilience.
4. **Verification of Facts:**
    - **Corroborating Information:** Ensuring the accuracy

of information by cross-referencing and verifying facts from multiple sources.
      - **Documenting Evidence:** Maintaining a trail of evidence to support claims and allegations.
5. **Whistleblower Protection:**
      - **Encouraging Whistleblowers:** Creating an environment that encourages individuals with insider information to come forward.
      - **Legal Protections:** Understanding and advocating for legal protections for whistleblowers.
6. **Story Framing:**
      - **Impactful Framing:** Presenting the story in a way that emphasizes its significance and potential impact on society.
      - **Public Interest:** Demonstrating that the investigation is in the public interest.
7. **Interviewing Skills:**
      - **Effective Questioning:** Conducting interviews with key stakeholders, experts, and individuals involved in the investigation.
      - **Gaining Trust:** Building trust with sources to encourage open and honest communication.
8. **Legal and Ethical Considerations:**
      - **Adherence to Legal Standards:** Operating within the boundaries of the law while pushing for transparency and accountability.
      - **Ethical Decision-Making:** Balancing the public's right to know with ethical considerations, such as privacy and potential harm.
9. **Data Journalism:**

- **Data Analysis:** Using data analysis and visualization tools to uncover patterns and trends.
- **Access to Information Laws:** Leveraging freedom of information laws to obtain relevant documents and data.

10. **Collaboration and Teamwork:**
    - **Collaborative Investigations:** Collaborating with other journalists or media organizations on large-scale investigative projects.
    - **Sharing Resources:** Pooling resources and expertise to enhance the depth and breadth of the investigation.

11. **Risk Assessment:**
    - **Security Measures:** Implementing security measures to protect journalists and sources, especially when dealing with sensitive or dangerous topics.
    - **Legal Risks:** Assessing potential legal risks and taking precautions to minimize legal challenges.

12. **Impact and Accountability:**
    - **Report Impact:** Evaluating the impact of the investigative report on public awareness, policy changes, or legal actions.
    - **Advocacy for Accountability:** Advocating for accountability and reform based on the findings of the investigation.

Investigative journalism plays a crucial role in democracy by bringing transparency, accountability, and social change. Despite its challenges, investigative journalists often uncover information that may not have come to light through routine reporting, contributing to the public's understanding of complex issues.

Digital Journalism

Digital journalism refers to the production, distribution, and consumption of news and information through digital platforms, including websites, social media, podcasts, mobile apps, and other online channels. Digital journalism has transformed the way news is created and consumed, offering new opportunities for storytelling, audience engagement, and real-time reporting. Here are key aspects and considerations in digital journalism:

1. **Online Platforms:**
   - **News Websites:** Publishing news articles, features, and multimedia content on dedicated news websites.
   - **Blogs:** Individual or collaborative online platforms where journalists share insights, opinions, and analysis.
   - **Aggregator Platforms:** Platforms that aggregate news content from various sources.
2. **Social Media Presence:**
   - **Social Media Reporting:** Using social media platforms for real-time updates, breaking news, and audience engagement.
   - **Community Building:** Building and engaging with a community of followers on platforms like Twitter, Facebook, and Instagram.
3. **Multimedia Storytelling:**
   - **Video Journalism:** Creating and sharing news stories through video content, interviews, and documentaries.

- **Infographics and Data Visualization:** Presenting complex information through visually appealing graphics and interactive charts.
- **Podcasting:** Producing audio content, including news briefs, interviews, and in-depth discussions.

4. **Mobile Journalism (MoJo):**
   - **On-the-Go Reporting:** Utilizing mobile devices for capturing photos, and videos, and conducting interviews.
   - **Mobile Editing Apps:** Editing and publishing content directly from smartphones and tablets.

5. **Audience Engagement:**
   - **Reader Comments and Feedback:** Encouraging audience participation through comments, feedback, and discussions.
   - **Social Media Interaction:** Engaging with the audience through social media platforms and responding to comments.

6. **Data Journalism:**
   - **Data Analysis:** Using data sets and analytics tools to uncover trends, patterns, and insights.
   - **Interactive Data Visualization:** Creating interactive graphics and charts to enhance data-driven storytelling.

7. **Real-Time Reporting:**
   - **Live Reporting:** Providing real-time updates and coverage of breaking news events.
   - **Live Streaming:** Using platforms like Facebook Live, YouTube Live, or Periscope for live video reporting.

8. **Search Engine Optimization (SEO):**
   - **SEO Best Practices:** Optimizing digital content for search engines to improve discoverability.
   - **Headline Writing for the Web:** Crafting compelling headlines that are both informative and attention-grabbing.
9. **Hyperlocal Journalism:**
   - **Community-Focused Reporting:** Covering news and events at the local level to serve specific communities.
   - **Collaboration with Local Businesses:** Partnering with local businesses and organizations for content and support.
10. **Agile Newsrooms:**
    - **Adaptability:** Adapting quickly to changes in the news landscape and audience preferences.
    - **Experimentation:** Trying out new formats, technologies, and storytelling techniques.
11. **User-Generated Content:**
    - **Crowdsourcing:** Involving the audience in the news-gathering process by seeking contributions, photos, and information.
    - **Verification of User-Generated Content:** Verifying and fact-checking content contributed by users.
12. **Monetization Strategies:**
    - **Digital Subscriptions:** Offering paid access to premium content.
    - **Advertising Revenue:** Generating revenue through digital advertising and sponsored content.

Digital journalism continues to evolve with advancements in technology, and journalists must navigate the digital landscape while upholding journalistic principles such as accuracy, fairness, and transparency. The digital era has democratized access to information, providing both opportunities and challenges for media organizations and journalists.

Chapter 3

Broadcasting

Broadcasting is the distribution of audio and video content to a widespread audience through electronic media, typically over the airwaves, through cable or satellite transmissions, or via the Internet. It encompasses various forms of media delivery, including television and radio broadcasting. Here are key aspects and considerations related to broadcasting:

1. **Television Broadcasting:**
   - **Terrestrial Television (Over-the-Air):** Transmission of television signals through antennas to receivers in homes.
   - **Cable and Satellite Television:** Delivery of television content through cable networks or satellite signals, providing a wider range of channels.
2. **Radio Broadcasting:**
   - **AM and FM Radio:** Different frequency bands for broadcasting audio content, including news, music, talk shows, and more.
   - **Digital Radio:** Broadcasting using digital technologies, providing higher sound quality and additional features.
3. **Broadcasting Studios:**
   - **Production Studios:** Facilities for creating and producing television and radio content, including news programs, shows, and commercials.
   - **Control Rooms:** Spaces equipped with technical infrastructure for managing live broadcasts, switching between cameras, and controlling audio.

4. **Transmission Towers:**
   - **Antenna Towers:** Structures used to transmit signals over the airwaves for reception by television and radio receivers.
   - **Satellite Transmission:** Broadcasting signals through satellites to reach a global audience.
5. **Live Broadcasting:**
   - **Live Events:** Broadcasting events, such as news, sports, concerts, and awards shows, in real-time.
   - **Live Interviews:** Conducting interviews and discussions on live broadcasts.
6. **Pre-recorded Content:**
   - **Produced Shows:** Creating and broadcasting pre-recorded content, including scripted shows, documentaries, and movies.
   - **Commercial Advertisements:** Airing pre-recorded advertisements during breaks in programming.
7. **News Broadcasting:**
   - **Newsrooms:** Facilities dedicated to gathering, producing, and disseminating news content.
   - **News Anchors and Reporters:** On-air personalities delivering news updates, reports, and analysis.
8. **Regulation and Licensing:**
   - **Government Oversight:** Broadcasting often falls under government regulations to ensure fair practices, adherence to standards, and protection of public interest.
   - **Licensing:** Obtaining licenses for broadcasting frequencies, subject to regulations and compliance.
9. **Digital Broadcasting:**

- **Digital Television (DTV):** Transition from analog to digital broadcasting for improved picture and sound quality.
- **Internet Streaming:** Broadcasting content over the internet through platforms like streaming services and online radio.

10. **Audience Measurement:**
    - **Ratings and Metrics:** Assessing audience size and demographics through ratings systems and analytics.
    - **Advertising Rates:** Determining advertising rates based on audience metrics and reach.

11. **Interactive Broadcasting:**
    - **Interactive Features:** Engaging the audience through interactive elements, such as social media integration, live polls, and viewer feedback.
    - **User-generated Content:** Encouraging viewers to contribute content or participate in discussions.

12. **Emerging Technologies:**
    - **Virtual and Augmented Reality:** Exploring new ways to enhance the viewer experience through immersive technologies.
    - **Artificial Intelligence:** Implementing AI for content recommendations, personalization, and data analysis.

Broadcasting serves as a powerful tool for disseminating information, entertainment, and cultural content to a broad audience. The transition to digital technologies has expanded the possibilities for content delivery and audience interaction, shaping the future landscape of broadcasting.

Radio Production

Radio production involves the planning, creation, and execution of audio content for broadcast on radio platforms. Whether producing music shows, talk programs, news broadcasts, or podcasts, radio production requires careful consideration of content, technical elements, and audience engagement. Here are key aspects and considerations in radio production:

1. **Pre-production:**
     - **Concept Development:** Defining the theme, format, and purpose of the radio show or program.
     - **Scriptwriting:** Preparing scripts for scripted segments, advertisements, and promotional content.
     - **Show Format:** Structuring the show with consideration for timing, segments, and flow.
2. **Content Planning:**
     - **Topic Selection:** Choosing relevant and engaging topics that align with the target audience.
     - **Guest Booking:** Identifying and scheduling guests for interviews or special segments.
     - **Music Selection:** Curating playlists or selecting music that complements the show's theme.
3. **Technical Planning:**
     - **Recording Logistics:** Determining whether the show will be recorded in a studio, remotely, or a combination of both.
     - **Sound Design:** Planning sound effects, jingles, and other audio elements to enhance the production.
     - **Technical Equipment:** Ensuring that audio

recording and broadcasting equipment is in good working order.

4. **Recording and Editing:**
   - **Recording Sessions:** Capturing live recordings, interviews, and voiceovers according to the script.
   - **Editing:** Refining and enhancing audio recordings through editing software.
   - **Mixing:** Balancing audio levels, adding effects, and ensuring a polished sound.

5. **Voice Performance:**
   - **Voice Talent:** Utilizing skilled and engaging hosts, presenters, and voiceover artists.
   - **Delivery Style:** Adapting delivery styles to suit the tone and format of the program.
   - **Pacing:** Maintaining an appropriate pace to keep the audience engaged.

6. **Live Broadcasting:**
   - **Live Shows:** Coordinating live broadcasts with precision in terms of timing, transitions, and audience interaction.
   - **Call-ins and Interactivity:** Managing live calls, messages, and other forms of audience participation.
   - **Technical Operations:** Ensuring smooth technical operations during live broadcasts.

7. **Post-production:**
   - **Final Editing:** Making additional edits, if necessary, after reviewing the recorded content.
   - **Adding Special Effects:** Incorporating post-production effects, transitions, and enhancements.
   - **Review and Approval:** Conducting a final review

before broadcasting or publishing.
8. **Promotions and Marketing:**
    - **Show Promotion:** Developing promotional materials for on-air and online promotion.
    - **Social Media Marketing:** Leveraging social media platforms to promote upcoming shows and engage with the audience.
    - **Cross-promotion:** Collaborating with other radio programs or platforms for mutual promotion.
9. **Scheduling and Coordination:**
    - **Broadcast Schedule:** Planning and adhering to a regular broadcasting schedule.
    - **Team Coordination:** Coordinating efforts among producers, hosts, technicians, and other team members.
10. **Compliance and Regulations:**
    - **Regulatory Compliance:** Ensuring adherence to broadcasting regulations, licensing requirements, and content standards.
    - **Copyright Compliance:** Obtaining proper permissions for music, interviews, and other copyrighted material.
11. **Feedback and Evaluation:**
    - **Audience Feedback:** Collecting and analyzing audience feedback through listener surveys, social media, and other channels.
    - **Show Evaluation:** Continuously assessing the success and effectiveness of each show for improvement.

Radio production is a dynamic and creative process that requires collaboration among various professionals, including producers, hosts, technicians, and marketing specialists. The goal is to create compelling and engaging content that resonates with the audience and meets the objectives of the program.

Television Production

Television production involves the planning, creation, and execution of audiovisual content for broadcast on television networks or streaming platforms. It encompasses a wide range of formats, including scripted shows, news programs, documentaries, reality TV, and more. Here are key aspects and considerations in television production:

1. **Pre-production:**
    - **Concept Development:** Defining the show's concept, theme, and target audience.
    - **Scriptwriting:** Developing scripts for episodes, including dialogue, narrative structure, and scene descriptions.
    - **Storyboarding:** Creating visual representations of scenes to guide the filming process.
    - **Casting:** Selecting actors and contributors for scripted shows or reality programs.
2. **Production Planning:**
    - **Budgeting:** Allocating resources, including funds, for the production.
    - **Scheduling:** Creating a timeline for pre-production, production, and post-production phases.
    - **Location Scouting:** Identifying and securing suitable filming locations.
    - **Technical Planning:** Deciding on camera equipment, lighting setups, and other technical aspects.
3. **Crew Selection:**
    - **Director:** Overseeing the creative and technical

aspects of the production.
- **Producers:** Managing various aspects, including budgeting, logistics, and coordination.
- **Cinematographer:** Managing camera work, framing, and visual aesthetics.
- **Production Designer:** Creating the visual look and feel of the show through set design and decoration.
- **Costume and Makeup Artists:** Ensuring appropriate attire and appearance for actors and contributors.

4. **Set Construction and Design:**
   - **Set Construction:** Building physical sets for scripted shows or talk programs.
   - **Set Decoration:** Adding props, furniture, and other elements to enhance the visual appeal.
   - **Lighting Design:** Planning and implementing lighting setups for optimal visibility and aesthetics.

5. **Filming (Production):**
   - **Principal Photography:** Capturing the main footage for each episode or segment.
   - **Direction of Actors:** Guiding actors and contributors to achieve the desired performances.
   - **Camera Operations:** Executing planned shots and angles for visual storytelling.

6. **Post-production:**
   - **Video Editing:** Assembling footage, adding special effects, and refining the visual narrative.
   - **Sound Design:** Enhancing audio quality, adding music, and incorporating sound effects.
   - **Color Correction:** Adjusting color tones and visual

elements for consistency.
- **Graphics and Animation:** Adding visual elements such as graphics, animations, and on-screen text.

7. **Quality Control:**
   - **Screening and Review:** Conducting internal screenings for quality assessment.
   - **Feedback and Revisions:** Making necessary adjustments based on feedback from producers and directors.

8. **Distribution:**
   - **Broadcast Delivery:** Transmitting the finished episodes to television networks for scheduled broadcasts.
   - **Streaming Platforms:** Preparing content for distribution on streaming services or online platforms.

9. **Promotion and Marketing:**
   - **Teaser Trailers:** Creating promotional trailers to generate interest and anticipation.
   - **Social Media Campaigns:** Leveraging social media for promotional activities and engaging with the audience.
   - **Press and Media Relations:** Collaborating with press outlets for interviews, reviews, and features.

10. **Audience Engagement:**
    - **Viewer Interaction:** Encouraging viewer engagement through social media, live events, and online forums.
    - **Contests and Promotions:** Running contests or promotions to attract and retain viewers.

11. **Compliance and Regulations:**
    - **Content Standards:** Ensuring adherence to broadcasting standards and content regulations.
    - **Clearances and Rights:** Securing legal clearances for music, footage, and other copyrighted material.

Television production is a collaborative and multifaceted process that involves a team of professionals working together to bring creative visions to life. It requires a balance of creativity, technical expertise, and effective project management to produce compelling and high-quality content for television audiences.

Broadcast Journalism

Broadcast journalism involves the production and dissemination of news and information through electronic media channels, such as television and radio. The goal is to inform the public about current events, issues, and developments through engaging and timely audiovisual storytelling. Here are key aspects and considerations in broadcast journalism:

1. **News Gathering:**
    - **Reporting:** Journalists collect information through interviews, research, and observation.
    - **Sources:** Establishing and cultivating reliable sources for accurate and timely information.
    - **Coverage Planning:** Deciding on the angle and focus of news stories.
2. **Scripting and Storytelling:**
    - **Scriptwriting:** Crafting scripts for news stories, ensuring clarity, conciseness, and journalistic standards.
    - **Narrative Structure:** Presenting information in a compelling and engaging narrative structure.
    - **Voiceover and Delivery:** Ensuring clear and articulate delivery by news anchors and reporters.
3. **Live Reporting:**
    - **Live Broadcasts:** Providing real-time updates during breaking news events or live reporting from the field.
    - **Field Reporting:** Conducting on-location interviews and reporting from the scene of events.

4. **Multimedia Storytelling:**
    - **Visual Elements:** Incorporating visuals such as video footage, images, and graphics to enhance storytelling.
    - **Graphics and Infographics:** Using visual aids to explain complex information or data.
    - **B-Roll Footage:** Supplementing news stories with additional footage for context and variety.
5. **Interviewing Skills:**
    - **Effective Questioning:** Asking clear, relevant, and probing questions during interviews.
    - **On-Air Interviews:** Conducting interviews on-air with newsmakers, experts, or eyewitnesses.
6. **Editing and Production:**
    - **Video Editing:** Assembling video footage, adding graphics, and ensuring visual coherence.
    - **Audio Editing:** Enhancing audio quality and balancing sound levels.
    - **Post-Production:** Finalizing news packages for broadcast.
7. **Newsroom Operations:**
    - **Editorial Meetings:** Collaborating with editors, producers, and other team members to plan coverage.
    - **Deadline Management:** Adhering to tight deadlines for news delivery.
    - **Breaking News Response:** Responding swiftly to breaking news with effective coverage plans.
8. **Media Ethics:**
    - **Accuracy and Fairness:** Ensuring news stories are

accurate, fair, and unbiased.
- **Conflict of Interest:** Avoiding conflicts of interest and maintaining journalistic integrity.
- **Privacy Considerations:** Respecting individuals' privacy rights while reporting on public issues.

9. **On-Air Presence:**
   - **News Anchors:** Presenting news stories with credibility, composure, and professionalism.
   - **Live Reporting Skills:** Conducting live reports with confidence and poise.

10. **Audience Engagement:**
    - **Viewer Interaction:** Encouraging viewer engagement through social media, feedback, and audience polls.
    - **Community Outreach:** Participating in community events and addressing local concerns.

11. **Legal Awareness:**
    - **Libel and Defamation:** Understanding and avoiding legal issues related to false and damaging statements.
    - **Freedom of the Press:** Upholding the principles of a free press while respecting legal boundaries.

12. **Adaptability to Technology:**
    - **Use of Digital Tools:** Leveraging digital tools for research, communication, and content creation.
    - **Mobile Journalism (MoJo):** Utilizing mobile devices for on-the-spot reporting and live broadcasts.

Broadcast journalism plays a crucial role in providing timely and accessible news coverage to a wide audience. It requires a combination of journalistic skills, technical expertise, and the ability to adapt to the fast-paced nature of the news industry.

Media Convergence

Media convergence refers to the merging of various media platforms, technologies, and industries to deliver content across multiple channels. It involves the integration of traditional and digital media forms, leading to the creation of new ways to produce, distribute, and consume information and entertainment. Here are key aspects and considerations related to media convergence:

1. **Integration of Technologies:**
    - **Digital Platforms:** The integration of digital technologies, including the internet, streaming services, and mobile devices, with traditional media forms such as television, radio, and print.
    - **Interactivity:** Enabling audiences to interact with content through social media, comments, and participatory platforms.
2. **Content Distribution:**
    - **Cross-Platform Distribution:** Delivering content seamlessly across various media platforms.
    - **Syndication:** Distributing content through multiple outlets, often simultaneously.
3. **Digitalization:**
    - **Digitization of Content:** Converting analog content into digital formats for wider accessibility.
    - **Digital Production:** Creating content directly in digital formats, facilitating editing, storage, and distribution.
4. **Convergence Devices:**
    - **Smart Devices:** The use of smart TVs, smartphones,

tablets, and other devices that bring together multiple forms of media and communication.
- **Connected Devices:** Devices that can access and display content from various sources, including streaming services and traditional broadcasts.

5. **Media Ownership and Consolidation:**
   - **Corporate Mergers:** The consolidation of media companies to create larger entities with diverse portfolios.
   - **Cross-Ownership:** Companies owning multiple types of media outlets, such as television stations, newspapers, and digital platforms.

6. **User-Generated Content:**
   - **Participatory Culture:** Users actively contribute content through blogs, social media, and online forums.
   - **Citizen Journalism:** Ordinary individuals reporting and sharing news through digital platforms.

7. **Technological Convergence:**
   - **Integrated Devices:** Combining functions of different devices into a single, multi-functional tool (e.g., smartphones with camera, video recorder, internet access).
   - **Common Platforms:** Platforms that support various types of media, like social media platforms hosting text, images, and videos.

8. **Economic and Business Models:**
   - **Subscription Services:** The rise of subscription-based models for accessing content, such as streaming services.

- **Advertising Revenue:** Platforms combining subscription models with advertising to generate revenue.
9. **Challenges and Opportunities:**
    - **Monetization Challenges:** The need for new revenue models as traditional advertising and subscription models evolve.
    - **Competition and Innovation:** Increased competition fosters innovation in content creation and distribution.
10. **Educational and Professional Impacts:**
    - **New Skill Sets:** The demand for professionals with skills in both traditional and digital media.
    - **Educational Adaptation:** Changes in media education to incorporate a broader range of skills and knowledge.
11. **Globalization of Content:**
    - **Global Reach:** Content reaching a worldwide audience through digital platforms.
    - **Cultural Impact:** Exposure to diverse cultural content from around the world.
12. **Regulatory Considerations:**
    - **Regulatory Challenges:** The need for updated regulations to address the changing landscape of media convergence.
    - **Net Neutrality:** Issues related to equal access to internet content without discrimination.

Media convergence has significantly transformed the media landscape, offering new opportunities for content creators, producers, and consumers. It has reshaped how information is accessed, shared, and consumed, blurring the boundaries between traditional media forms and creating a more interconnected and dynamic media ecosystem.

Chapter 4

Public Relations

Public relations (PR) is a strategic communication discipline that focuses on building and maintaining positive relationships between an organization and its various stakeholders. The goal of public relations is to create a positive image and reputation for the organization, manage perceptions, and communicate effectively with the public. Here are key aspects and considerations in public relations:

1. **Strategic Planning:**
   - **Objectives:** Establishing clear and measurable PR goals aligned with the organization's overall objectives.
   - **Audience Identification:** Identifying and understanding the target audience and key stakeholders.
2. **Media Relations:**
   - **Press Releases:** Creating and distributing press releases to announce news, events, or organizational updates.
   - **Media Outreach:** Building relationships with journalists, editors, and media outlets to secure positive coverage.
   - **Crisis Communication:** Developing strategies for addressing and managing crises or negative publicity.
3. **Content Creation:**
   - **Storytelling:** Crafting compelling narratives to engage and connect with the audience.
   - **Content Marketing:** Creating and sharing valuable content to enhance the organization's reputation.

- **Blogs and Articles:** Writing articles and blog posts to showcase expertise and thought leadership.
4. **Social Media Management:**
    - **Social Media Strategy:** Developing a strategic approach to social media to enhance brand visibility and engagement.
    - **Community Building:** Fostering relationships with online communities and responding to feedback.
    - **Social Listening:** Monitoring social media channels for mentions, trends, and sentiments.
5. **Event Planning and Management:**
    - **Event Coordination:** Planning and executing events to promote products, initiatives, or brand awareness.
    - **Sponsorships:** Identifying and securing relevant sponsorships to increase visibility.
6. **Internal Communications:**
    - **Employee Communications:** Keeping employees informed and engaged with organizational news and updates.
    - **Internal Campaigns:** Running internal campaigns to promote company culture and values.
7. **Public Affairs:**
    - **Government Relations:** Engaging with government entities to influence public policy or address regulatory issues.
    - **Advocacy Campaigns:** Developing campaigns to promote social or political causes aligned with the organization's values.
8. **Brand Management:**

- **Brand Messaging:** Crafting consistent and compelling messaging to reinforce the brand identity.
- **Brand Positioning:** Positioning the organization as a leader in its industry or field.

9. **Measurement and Evaluation:**
   - **Metrics and Analytics:** Monitoring and analyzing PR efforts using key performance indicators (KPIs).
   - **Media Monitoring:** Tracking media coverage and sentiment to assess the impact of PR campaigns.

10. **Community Relations:**
    - **Community Engagement:** Establishing relationships with local communities through outreach and involvement.
    - **Corporate Social Responsibility (CSR):** Demonstrating commitment to social and environmental causes.

11. **Ethical Considerations:**
    - **Transparency:** Communicating openly and honestly with stakeholders.
    - **Integrity:** Upholding ethical standards in all communications and actions.

12. **Adaptability and Crisis Management:**
    - **Flexibility:** Adapting strategies to changing circumstances and trends.
    - **Crisis Preparedness:** Developing crisis communication plans to address unforeseen challenges.

Public relations professionals play a vital role in shaping public perception, managing reputations, and fostering positive relationships between organizations and their stakeholders. Effective public relations involve a combination of strategic planning, communication skills, and the ability to adapt to evolving media landscapes.

PR Strategies

Public relations (PR) strategies are carefully planned and executed approaches to building and managing relationships between an organization and its various stakeholders. These strategies aim to create a positive image, enhance reputation, and effectively communicate with the public. Here are key PR strategies commonly employed by organizations:

1. **Define Clear Objectives:**
    - Establish specific and measurable PR goals aligned with the overall organizational objectives.
    - Clearly define what the organization aims to achieve through its PR efforts, such as increased brand awareness, improved reputation, or successful product launches.
2. **Target Audience Identification:**
    - Identify and understand the key stakeholders and target audience.
    - Tailor messages and communication channels to effectively reach and engage with the intended audience.
3. **Craft Compelling Storytelling:**
    - Develop compelling narratives that resonate with the target audience.
    - Use storytelling to humanize the organization, showcase its values, and create an emotional connection with stakeholders.
4. **Media Relations:**
    - Build and maintain positive relationships with journalists, editors, and media outlets.
    - Distribute press releases, organize media events, and

respond promptly to media inquiries.
- Position organizational spokespeople as industry experts for media interviews and commentary.

5. **Digital and Social Media Strategy:**
   - Develop a comprehensive digital and social media strategy to enhance online presence.
   - Utilize social media platforms for engaging content, community building, and real-time communication.
   - Implement online reputation management to monitor and respond to mentions and comments.

6. **Crisis Communication Planning:**
   - Develop a crisis communication plan that outlines protocols and procedures for responding to crises.
   - Conduct crisis simulations and training to ensure the team is prepared to handle unexpected challenges.

7. **Employee Communications:**
   - Keep employees informed about organizational updates, achievements, and changes.
   - Foster internal communication channels to encourage dialogue and feedback.
   - Empower employees to be brand ambassadors.

8. **Content Marketing:**
   - Create and share valuable content that positions the organization as a thought leader.
   - Utilize blogs, articles, whitepapers, and multimedia content to convey expertise and insights.
   - Align content with organizational values and industry trends.

9. **Events and Sponsorships:**
   - Plan and execute events that align with organizational goals and target audiences.

- Identify relevant sponsorships that enhance brand visibility and credibility.

10. **Community Engagement:**
    - Establish and maintain positive relationships with local communities.
    - Engage in corporate social responsibility (CSR) initiatives that align with community needs and values.

11. **Measurement and Evaluation:**
    - Set key performance indicators (KPIs) to measure the success of PR efforts.
    - Regularly evaluate and analyze PR metrics, such as media coverage, audience engagement, and sentiment.

12. **Adaptability and Continuous Improvement:**
    - Stay agile and adapt strategies to changing circumstances, industry trends, and stakeholder expectations.
    - Continuously gather feedback and assess the effectiveness of PR initiatives for ongoing improvement.

13. **Collaboration and Partnerships:**
    - Collaborate with other organizations, influencers, or industry leaders to amplify messages and reach a wider audience.
    - Form strategic partnerships that align with organizational values and objectives.

By incorporating these strategies, organizations can effectively manage their public relations efforts, build positive relationships with stakeholders, and navigate the complex landscape of communication in today's dynamic business environment.

Crisis Communication

Crisis communication is a specialized area of public relations focused on managing and mitigating the impact of unexpected and potentially damaging events or situations that could harm an organization's reputation. The goal is to effectively communicate with key stakeholders, address concerns, and navigate the crisis while minimizing reputational damage. Here are key principles and strategies for crisis communication:

1. **Preparedness and Planning:**
   - **Establish a Crisis Communication Team:** Designate a team responsible for managing communication during a crisis, including spokespersons, PR professionals, legal advisors, and relevant stakeholders.
   - **Develop a Crisis Communication Plan:** Create a comprehensive plan that outlines roles, responsibilities, communication protocols, and response strategies for different types of crises.
2. **Early Detection and Monitoring:**
   - **Monitor for Potential Crises:** Use media monitoring tools and social listening to detect early signs of potential crises.
   - **Establish Warning Systems:** Set up mechanisms to identify issues early, both internally and externally.
3. **Transparent and Timely Communication:**
   - **Openness and Honesty:** Be transparent and honest about the situation. Provide accurate information, acknowledging what is known and, if necessary,

what is still being investigated.
- **Timely Response:** Respond quickly to address the crisis, demonstrating a commitment to addressing the issue and providing regular updates.

4. **Choose the Right Spokesperson:**
   - **Media-Trained Spokespersons:** Designate individuals who are trained in crisis communication as official spokespeople.
   - **Authority and Credibility:** Choose spokespersons with the authority and credibility to address the specific crisis.

5. **Audience-Centric Communication:**
   - **Understand Audience Concerns:** Identify the concerns and needs of different stakeholder groups, including customers, employees, investors, and the public.
   - **Tailor Messages:** Tailor messages to address specific concerns and reassure stakeholders.

6. **Consistent Messaging:**
   - **Consistency Across Channels:** Ensure consistent messaging across all communication channels, including traditional media, social media, and internal communication.
   - **Unified Front:** Present a unified front among leadership and team members to avoid mixed messages.

7. **Active Listening and Feedback:**
   - **Engage with Stakeholders:** Actively listen to concerns from stakeholders and address their questions or comments.

- **Feedback Loops:** Establish feedback mechanisms to continually assess the effectiveness of communication strategies.

8. **Use of Social Media:**
   - **Real-Time Updates:** Leverage social media for real-time updates and engagement with the public.
   - **Monitoring and Response:** Monitor social media channels for misinformation and respond promptly to correct inaccuracies.

9. **Legal Considerations:**
   - **Legal Counsel Involvement:** Involve legal counsel to navigate potential legal implications and ensure compliance with regulations.
   - **Careful Language Use:** Choose language carefully to avoid admissions of guilt or liability.

10. **Recovery and Rebuilding:**
    - **Post-Crisis Communication:** Develop a post-crisis communication plan to rebuild trust and reputation.
    - **Highlight Corrective Actions:** Communicate the steps taken to address the issue and prevent recurrence.

11. **Training and Simulation Exercises:**
    - **Crisis Drills:** Conduct regular training exercises and simulations to prepare the crisis communication team for various scenarios.
    - **Continuous Improvement:** Use post-crisis evaluations to identify areas for improvement in crisis communication strategies.

12. **Empathy and Apology:**
    - **Express Empathy:** Demonstrate empathy towards

those affected by the crisis, acknowledging their concerns and feelings.
- **Apologize when Appropriate:** If the organization is at fault, offer a sincere apology and outline corrective actions.

Crisis communication is a dynamic process that requires a proactive and strategic approach to safeguard an organization's reputation during challenging times. By following these principles and strategies, organizations can navigate crises more effectively and work towards restoring trust with stakeholders.

Corporate Communication

Corporate communication is a comprehensive function within an organization that focuses on managing and facilitating effective communication both internally and externally. It involves conveying consistent messages, building relationships, and shaping the organization's reputation. Here are key elements and considerations in corporate communication:

1. **Internal Communication:**
    - **Employee Communication:** Keeping employees informed about organizational goals, changes, and updates.
    - **Intranet and Internal Platforms:** Utilizing digital platforms for internal communication, including company intranets, newsletters, and messaging apps.
    - **Town Hall Meetings:** Conducting regular meetings to update employees and encourage open dialogue.
2. **External Communication:**
    - **Media Relations:** Building relationships with journalists and managing media inquiries.
    - **Public Relations:** Managing the organization's image and reputation through strategic communication.
    - **Community Relations:** Engaging with and contributing to the local community, demonstrating corporate social responsibility (CSR).
3. **Brand Communication:**
    - **Brand Messaging:** Developing and maintaining consistent messaging to reinforce the organization's

brand identity.
- **Visual Identity:** Ensuring a cohesive visual identity in branding materials, including logos, colors, and design elements.

4. **Crisis Communication:**
   - **Crisis Planning:** Developing plans and protocols for effective communication during crises.
   - **Spokesperson Training:** Ensuring designated spokespeople are prepared and trained for crisis communication.
   - **Reputation Management:** Implementing strategies to protect and enhance the organization's reputation.

5. **Corporate Social Responsibility (CSR):**
   - **CSR Communication:** Communicating the organization's commitment to social responsibility and sustainability.
   - **Reporting and Transparency:** Sharing information on CSR initiatives and progress transparently with stakeholders.

6. **Investor Relations:**
   - **Financial Communication:** Providing transparent and accurate financial information to investors and shareholders.
   - **Annual Reports:** Creating comprehensive reports outlining financial performance, strategic initiatives, and corporate governance.

7. **Leadership Communication:**
   - **Executive Communication:** Ensuring leaders effectively communicate with internal and external

audiences.
- **Thought Leadership:** Positioning executives as thought leaders in their respective industries through articles, speaking engagements, and industry contributions.

8. **Digital Communication:**
   - **Social Media Management:** Engaging with audiences on social media platforms to build brand presence and connect with stakeholders.
   - **Online Presence:** Maintaining an updated and user-friendly website with relevant content.
   - **Email Communication:** Utilizing email for targeted communication with various stakeholders.

9. **Employee Advocacy:**
   - **Encouraging Employee Advocacy:** Empowering employees to be ambassadors for the organization.
   - **Internal Influencers:** Identifying and leveraging employees with influence within the organization.

10. **Change Communication:**
    - **Change Management Communication:** Communicating effectively during organizational changes, mergers, or restructurings.
    - **Employee Engagement:** Ensuring employees understand and support organizational changes.

11. **Metrics and Evaluation:**
    - **Key Performance Indicators (KPIs):** Establishing and monitoring KPIs to measure the effectiveness of corporate communication.
    - **Surveys and Feedback:** Gathering feedback from internal and external stakeholders through surveys

and other feedback mechanisms.
12. **Ethical Communication:**
    - **Adherence to Ethical Standards:** Ensuring all communication aligns with ethical principles and standards.
    - **Transparency:** Being transparent and honest in communication, especially during challenging situations.

Corporate communication is an integral part of organizational success, contributing to the building of a positive corporate culture, effective stakeholder relations, and a strong brand presence in the market. A well-managed corporate communication strategy helps align internal and external messaging, fostering trust and credibility.

Reputation Management

Reputation management is a strategic process of building, maintaining, and protecting an individual's or organization's image and perception in the eyes of various stakeholders. It involves proactive efforts to shape public opinion positively and reactive measures to address challenges that may affect reputation. Here are key elements and strategies in reputation management:

1. **Monitoring and Listening:**
   - **Media Monitoring:** Use tools to monitor traditional and digital media for mentions of the individual or organization.
   - **Social Media Monitoring:** Keep track of conversations, comments, and mentions on social media platforms.
   - **Online Reviews:** Monitor and manage reviews on websites, forums, and review platforms.
2. **Understand Stakeholder Perceptions:**
   - **Identify Key Stakeholders:** Determine the groups and individuals that significantly influence the reputation.
   - **Conduct Surveys and Feedback:** Gather feedback from stakeholders to understand their perceptions and expectations.
3. **Develop a Strong Brand Image:**
   - **Consistent Branding:** Ensure a consistent visual and messaging identity across all communication channels.
   - **Showcase Achievements:** Highlight positive

achievements, awards, and contributions.
- **Thought Leadership:** Establish the individual or organization as an authority in their field through thought leadership content.

4. **Crisis Preparedness:**
   - **Develop a Crisis Communication Plan:** Prepare for potential crises by having a well-defined communication plan.
   - **Spokesperson Training:** Train key spokespersons to handle crisis communication effectively.

5. **Transparency and Open Communication:**
   - **Open and Honest Communication:** Be transparent about achievements, challenges, and any issues.
   - **Apologize and Correct Mistakes:** If mistakes occur, acknowledge them, apologize, and take corrective actions.

6. **Online Reputation Management:**
   - **Search Engine Optimization (SEO):** Optimize online content to ensure positive and accurate information appears prominently in search results.
   - **Content Creation:** Create and publish positive content on owned platforms and third-party websites.

7. **Engage with Stakeholders:**
   - **Social Media Engagement:** Actively engage with the audience on social media, respond to comments, and address concerns.
   - **Community Involvement:** Participate in community activities and initiatives to enhance

positive relationships.

8. **Customer Relationship Management (CRM):**
   - **Customer Satisfaction:** Focus on delivering quality products or services to ensure customer satisfaction.
   - **Handle Complaints Effectively:** Address customer complaints promptly and professionally.

9. **Legal Considerations:**
   - **Intellectual Property Protection:** Protect intellectual property to prevent misuse or unauthorized use.
   - **Compliance with Regulations:** Ensure compliance with legal and regulatory standards in all communications.

10. **Employee Advocacy:**
    - **Employee Training:** Train employees on the importance of maintaining a positive online presence.
    - **Encourage Positive Employee Engagement:** Foster a positive workplace culture that encourages employees to be advocates for the organization.

11. **Regular Audits and Assessments:**
    - **Reputation Audits:** Periodically assess the current state of reputation through audits and assessments.
    - **Adjust Strategies as Needed:** Based on assessments, adjust reputation management strategies to address emerging challenges or opportunities.

12. **Media Relations:**
    - **Build Positive Media Relations:** Cultivate positive relationships with journalists and media outlets.
    - **Press Releases and Positive Stories:** Regularly issue

press releases highlighting positive achievements and stories.
13. **Educate and Communicate Values:**
    - **Communicate Organizational Values:** Clearly articulate and communicate the values that guide the organization.
    - **Educate Stakeholders:** Educate stakeholders about the organization's mission, vision, and ethical principles.

Reputation management is an ongoing and multifaceted process that requires a combination of proactive efforts to build a positive image and reactive strategies to address challenges. By consistently monitoring, engaging, and communicating effectively, individuals and organizations can strengthen and protect their reputations over time.

Chapter 5

Advertising

Advertising is a form of communication that aims to promote or sell a product, service, idea, or brand to a target audience. It involves creating and disseminating persuasive messages through various channels to influence consumer behavior. Here are key elements and considerations in advertising:

1. **Advertising Objectives:**
    - **Awareness:** Introducing a new product, service, or brand to the target audience.
    - **Consideration:** Encouraging consumers to consider the advertised product or service.
    - **Conversion:** Convincing consumers to take a specific action, such as making a purchase.
2. **Target Audience:**
    - **Define the Target Market:** Identify the demographic, psychographic, and behavioral characteristics of the audience.
    - **Tailor Messages:** Create messages that resonate with the specific interests and preferences of the target audience.
3. **Advertising Channels:**
    - **Traditional Media:** Utilize traditional advertising channels such as television, radio, newspapers, and magazines.
    - **Digital Media:** Leverage online platforms, including social media, websites, search engines, and email.
    - **Outdoor Advertising:** Use billboards, transit ads,

and other outdoor mediums for visibility.
- **Print Advertising:** Publish ads in print publications like magazines, newspapers, and brochures.

4. **Creative Elements:**
   - **Message Content:** Craft compelling and memorable messages that communicate the value proposition.
   - **Visual Design:** Use visuals, such as images, graphics, and videos, to enhance the visual appeal.
   - **Copywriting:** Develop persuasive and concise written content that captures attention.

5. **Call to Action (CTA):**
   - **Encourage Action:** Communicate what action the audience should take after seeing the advertisement.
   - **Create Urgency:** Use time-sensitive language to prompt immediate responses.

6. **Budgeting:**
   - **Set Advertising Budget:** Determine the financial resources allocated to advertising campaigns.
   - **Cost Considerations:** Evaluate the costs associated with different advertising channels and creative production.

7. **Media Planning:**
   - **Selecting Media Channels:** Choose the most appropriate channels based on the target audience, campaign goals, and budget.
   - **Media Buying:** Negotiate and purchase advertising space or time in selected media channels.

8. **Campaign Evaluation:**
   - **Metrics and KPIs:** Establish key performance

indicators (KPIs) to measure the success of the advertising campaign.
- **Analytics:** Use analytics tools to track and analyze the performance of digital advertising campaigns.

9. **Ad Testing:**
    - **A/B Testing:** Experiment with different ad variations to identify the most effective elements.
    - **Focus Groups:** Gather feedback from focus groups to assess the impact and reception of ads.

10. **Brand Consistency:**
    - **Maintain Consistent Branding:** Ensure that advertising materials align with the overall brand identity.
    - **Brand Messaging:** Consistently communicate the brand's values, personality, and unique selling points.

11. **Regulatory Compliance:**
    - **Adherence to Laws and Guidelines:** Ensure that advertising content complies with legal and ethical standards.
    - **Industry Regulations:** Be aware of industry-specific regulations and guidelines.

12. **Adapting to Trends:**
    - **Stay Current:** Keep abreast of advertising trends and consumer behavior.
    - **Incorporate New Technologies:** Explore innovative technologies, such as augmented reality or interactive ads, to enhance engagement.

13. **Global Considerations:**
    - **Cultural Sensitivity:** Tailor advertisements to be

culturally sensitive and relevant in diverse markets.
- **Localization:** Consider adapting content to local languages and customs for global campaigns.

Advertising is a dynamic field that requires strategic planning, creativity, and adaptability. Effective advertising campaigns aim to capture attention, create emotional connections, and drive desired actions among the target audience. The combination of a well-defined strategy, compelling creative elements, and a thorough understanding of the audience contributes to the success of advertising efforts.

Advertising Strategies

Advertising strategies are carefully planned approaches used by businesses and organizations to promote their products, services, or brands to a target audience. Effective advertising strategies involve a combination of creativity, market research, and strategic planning. Here are some common advertising strategies:

1. **Target Audience Identification:**
    - **Define Your Target Audience:** Identify the demographic, psychographic, and behavioral characteristics of the audience you want to reach.
    - **Segmentation:** Break down the target audience into smaller segments for more personalized and effective messaging.
2. **Clear Value Proposition:**
    - **Communicate Unique Selling Points (USPs):** Clearly articulate what sets your product or service apart from competitors.
    - **Highlight Benefits:** Emphasize the benefits that consumers will gain from choosing your offering.
3. **Emotional Appeal:**
    - **Create Emotional Connections:** Develop ads that evoke emotions and connect with the audience on a personal level.
    - **Storytelling:** Use storytelling techniques to make the brand or product relatable and memorable.
4. **Consistent Branding:**
    - **Maintain Brand Consistency:** Ensure that all advertising materials align with the overall brand

identity.
- **Visual Identity:** Use consistent colors, logos, and design elements to reinforce brand recognition.

5. **Multi-Channel Marketing:**
    - **Utilize Various Platforms:** Employ a mix of traditional and digital advertising channels, including TV, radio, social media, online display ads, and email.
    - **Integrated Campaigns:** Coordinate messaging across different channels for a cohesive brand presence.

6. **Influencer Marketing:**
    - **Collaborate with Influencers:** Partner with influencers who align with your brand to reach their followers.
    - **Authentic Endorsements:** Ensure influencer endorsements appear genuine and align with the influencer's audience.

7. **Limited-Time Offers and Promotions:**
    - **Create a Sense of Urgency:** Use limited-time offers, discounts, or promotions to encourage immediate action.
    - **Flash Sales:** Introduce flash sales or exclusive deals to attract attention and drive sales.

8. **Interactive and Engaging Content:**
    - **Interactive Ads:** Develop ads that encourage audience interaction, such as quizzes, polls, or games.
    - **User-Generated Content (UGC):** Encourage customers to create and share content related to

your brand.

9. **Search Engine Marketing (SEM):**
    - **Pay-per-click (PPC):** Use paid search advertising to appear at the top of search engine results for relevant keywords.
    - **Search Engine Optimization (SEO):** Optimize website content to improve organic search rankings.
10. **Remarketing:**
    - **Retargeting Ads:** Display ads to users who have previously visited your website but did not make a purchase.
    - **Personalized Recommendations:** Provide personalized recommendations based on users' previous interactions.
11. **Testimonials and Reviews:**
    - **Customer Testimonials:** Showcase positive customer experiences through testimonials and reviews.
    - **Third-Party Endorsements:** Highlight awards, certifications, or positive mentions from reputable sources.
12. **Mobile Advertising:**
    - **Mobile-Friendly Ads:** Design ads that are optimized for mobile devices.
    - **Location-Based Advertising:** Utilize location-based targeting for relevant and timely messages.
13. **Sustainability and Social Responsibility:**
    - **Green Marketing:** Highlight environmentally friendly practices and initiatives.
    - **Corporate Social Responsibility (CSR):**

Communicate social responsibility efforts to resonate with socially conscious consumers.

14. **Data-Driven Targeting:**
    - **Utilize Data Analytics:** Analyze consumer data to understand behaviors and preferences.
    - **Targeted Advertising:** Use data-driven insights to target specific audience segments with tailored messages.

15. **Measuring and Analyzing Results:**
    - **Key Performance Indicators (KPIs):** Establish measurable goals and metrics to evaluate the success of advertising campaigns.
    - **Analytics Tools:** Use analytics tools to track and analyze campaign performance, user engagement, and conversions.

Successful advertising strategies are dynamic and responsive to changes in consumer behavior, market trends, and industry landscapes. A well-executed advertising campaign considers the unique characteristics of the target audience and leverages creative and data-driven approaches to achieve its objectives. Regular evaluation and adjustments based on performance metrics contribute to ongoing campaign success.

Consumer Behavior

Consumer behavior refers to the study of the processes and activities individuals engage in when searching for, purchasing, using, evaluating, and disposing of products and services. Understanding consumer behavior is crucial for businesses and marketers as it helps them anticipate and respond to the needs, preferences, and decision-making processes of their target audience. Here are key factors and concepts related to consumer behavior:

1. **Motivation:**
    - **Needs and Wants:** Consumers are motivated by both physiological needs (necessities) and psychological wants (desires and aspirations).
    - **Maslow's Hierarchy of Needs:** The theory suggests that individuals prioritize fulfilling basic needs before moving on to higher-level needs like social belonging, esteem, and self-actualization.
2. **Perception:**
    - **Selective Attention:** Consumers focus on certain stimuli and ignore others.
    - **Perceptual Filters:** Personal experiences, attitudes, and beliefs shape how individuals perceive and interpret information.
3. **Learning:**
    - **Behavioral Learning:** Consumers acquire new behaviors through experiences, such as conditioning and reinforcement.
    - **Cognitive Learning:** Consumers gain knowledge and understanding through thinking, problem-

solving, and information processing.

4. **Attitudes and Beliefs:**
   - **Attitudes:** Long-term evaluations or feelings about a product, service, or brand.
   - **Beliefs:** Consumers' subjective assessments of a product's attributes and benefits.

5. **Personality and Lifestyle:**
   - **Personality Traits:** Individual characteristics that influence behavior, such as extroversion or conscientiousness.
   - **Lifestyle:** A person's patterns of living, including activities, interests, and opinions, which shape purchasing decisions.

6. **Social Influence:**
   - **Reference Groups:** Social groups that influence consumer behavior, including family, friends, and colleagues.
   - **Social Class:** The hierarchical division of society based on factors like income, education, and occupation.

7. **Cultural Factors:**
   - **Culture:** Shared values, beliefs, customs, and behaviors passed down from generation to generation.
   - **Subculture:** Smaller groups within a culture that share distinct characteristics.

8. **Decision-Making Process:**
   - **Problem Recognition:** Identifying a need or problem that prompts the decision-making process.
   - **Information Search:** Gathering information about

available options.
- **Evaluation of Alternatives:** Assessing the pros and cons of different products or services.
- **Purchase Decision:** Selecting a product or service based on evaluation.
- **Post-Purchase Evaluation:** Reflecting on the decision and assessing satisfaction or dissatisfaction.

9. **Consumer Segmentation:**
    - **Demographic Segmentation:** Grouping consumers based on demographic factors like age, gender, income, and education.
    - **Psychographic Segmentation:** Categorizing consumers based on lifestyle, values, and attitudes.

10. **Online Consumer Behavior:**
    - **E-Commerce:** The study of consumer behavior in online purchasing environments.
    - **Social Media Influence:** The impact of social media platforms on product discovery, recommendations, and reviews.

11. **Brand Loyalty and Trust:**
    - **Brand Loyalty:** Consumers' commitment to repeatedly purchasing a particular brand.
    - **Trust:** The belief that a brand will consistently deliver on its promises and meet expectations.

12. **Influencers and Word of Mouth:**
    - **Influencer Marketing:** Leveraging individuals with influence to promote products or services.
    - **Word of Mouth:** Recommendations and information spread by consumers to others.

13. **Cognitive Dissonance:**

- **Post-Purchase Dissonance:** Feelings of discomfort or doubt after a purchase, prompting consumers to seek reassurance.

14. **Consumer Decision-Making Models:**
    - **Howard-Sheth Model:** A comprehensive model that considers various factors influencing consumer decisions, including external influences, internal processes, and post-purchase behavior.
    - **Engel-Kollat-Blackwell Model:** Emphasizes the iterative nature of the decision-making process, with consumers continually gathering information and reassessing choices.

15. **Ethical and Sustainable Consumption:**
    - **Ethical Considerations:** The impact of ethical practices, such as fair trade or environmentally friendly production, on consumer choices.
    - **Sustainable Consumption:** The growing interest in products and brands that prioritize environmental and social responsibility.

Understanding consumer behavior is an ongoing process that requires businesses and marketers to adapt to changing trends, preferences, and societal influences. By gaining insights into consumer motivations and decision-making processes, organizations can tailor their marketing strategies to effectively meet the needs and expectations of their target audience.

Copywriting

Copywriting is the art and science of writing persuasive and compelling content, known as "copy," to promote a product, service, idea, or brand. Copywriting aims to engage the audience, create awareness, and ultimately drive a desired action, such as making a purchase or signing up for a newsletter. Effective copywriting involves a deep understanding of the target audience, the product or service being promoted, and the desired outcome. Here are key elements and considerations in copywriting:

1. **Know Your Audience:**
   - **Audience Persona:** Create detailed profiles of your target audience, considering demographics, interests, and motivations.
   - **Understand Pain Points:** Identify the challenges and needs of your audience to address them in your copy.
2. **Craft a Compelling Headline:**
   - **Capture Attention:** The headline should grab the reader's attention and entice them to continue reading.
   - **Clear and Concise:** Keep headlines clear, concise, and relevant to the content that follows.
3. **Focus on Benefits, Not Features:**
   - **Highlight Value:** Emphasize how the product or service solves a problem or improves the customer's life.
   - **Use Persuasive Language:** Convey the benefits in a way that resonates emotionally with the audience.
4. **Create a Strong Call to Action (CTA):**

- **Clear and Direct:** Clearly instruct the reader on what action to take, whether it's making a purchase, signing up, or contacting.
- **Urgency and Persuasion:** Use language that creates a sense of urgency or emphasizes the benefits of taking immediate action.

5. **Tell a Story:**
   - **Narrative Structure:** Weave a compelling story that connects with the audience on an emotional level.
   - **Relatable Characters:** Introduce relatable characters or scenarios that resonate with the target audience.

6. **Use Persuasive Language:**
   - **Powerful Words:** Employ words that evoke emotion and create a strong impact.
   - **Positive Tone:** Maintain an optimistic tone to inspire confidence and enthusiasm.

7. **Maintain Clarity:**
   - **Simplicity:** Keep the copy clear and simple to ensure easy comprehension.
   - **Avoid Jargon:** Minimize the use of industry-specific jargon that may confuse the audience.

8. **Build Credibility:**
   - **Testimonials and Reviews:** Incorporate customer testimonials or reviews to build trust.
   - **Statistics and Data:** Use relevant data or statistics to support claims and build credibility.

9. **Address Objections:**
   - **Anticipate Concerns:** Consider potential objections or doubts your audience may have and

address them in the copy.
- **Provide Solutions:** Offer solutions to common concerns to alleviate hesitations.

10. **Create Scannable Content:**
    - **Subheadings and Bullets:** Break up the content with subheadings, bullet points, and short paragraphs for easy readability.
    - **Highlight Key Information:** Emphasize important points using bold text or italics.

11. **SEO Optimization:**
    - **Keyword Research:** Incorporate relevant keywords to improve search engine visibility.
    - **Natural Integration:** Ensure keywords are seamlessly integrated into the copy for a natural flow.

12. **Test and Iterate:**
    - **A/B Testing:** Experiment with different versions of your copy to determine what resonates best with your audience.
    - **Analytics:** Use analytics tools to track performance and make data-driven improvements.

13. **Adapt to the Platform:**
    - **Platform-Specific Strategies:** Tailor your copy to the platform where it will be displayed (e.g., website, social media, email).
    - **Consider User Behavior:** Understand how users engage with content on specific platforms and adapt your approach accordingly.

Copywriting is a dynamic and evolving field that requires creativity, empathy, and a deep understanding of consumer behavior. Effective copy resonates with the audience, communicates a clear message, and motivates them to take action. Whether in digital marketing, print advertising, or other communication channels, compelling copywriting is a cornerstone of successful promotional efforts.

Branding

Branding is a strategic process of creating and managing a distinctive identity for a product, service, or organization to build recognition, trust, and loyalty among target audiences. A strong brand encompasses various elements that collectively shape the way a brand is perceived by consumers. Here are key components and considerations in branding:

1. **Brand Identity:**
    - **Brand Name:** A distinctive and memorable name that represents the brand.
    - **Logo:** A visual symbol or mark that serves as a recognizable identifier.
    - **Tagline or Slogan:** A brief and memorable phrase that encapsulates the brand's essence or value proposition.
2. **Brand Image:**
    - **Perception:** How the brand is perceived by consumers, including associations, emotions, and attributes.
    - **Brand Personality:** The human traits and characteristics attributed to the brand, creating a more relatable image.
3. **Brand Positioning:**
    - **Differentiation:** Clearly defining what sets the brand apart from competitors.
    - **Target Audience:** Identifying the specific market segment the brand aims to serve.
    - **Value Proposition:** Articulating the unique value and benefits the brand offers to consumers.

4. **Brand Equity:**
   - **Brand Recognition:** The level of awareness and familiarity consumers have with the brand.
   - **Brand Loyalty:** The degree to which customers remain committed to and consistently choose the brand over alternatives.
   - **Perceived Quality:** The consumer's assessment of the brand's quality and value.
5. **Consistent Branding:**
   - **Visual Consistency:** Maintaining a consistent visual identity across all brand elements.
   - **Messaging Consistency:** Ensuring that brand messages align with the overall brand positioning and values.
6. **Brand Communication:**
   - **Integrated Marketing Communications (IMC):** Coordinating consistent messaging across various communication channels.
   - **Storytelling:** Creating and sharing narratives that convey the brand's history, values, and mission.
   - **Emotional Connection:** Building emotional ties with consumers through relatable and authentic communication.
7. **Brand Experience:**
   - **Customer Touchpoints:** Identifying and optimizing every interaction a customer has with the brand.
   - **Customer Service:** Providing a positive and consistent experience through customer support and service.

8. **Brand Extensions:**
    - **Product Line Extensions:** Expanding the brand by introducing new products or services.
    - **Brand Stretching:** Extending the brand into new markets or categories.
9. **Brand Guidelines:**
    - **Style Guide:** A set of rules and standards that govern the use of brand elements to maintain consistency.
    - **Brand Manual:** Documentation outlining the brand's values, personality, and guidelines for internal and external stakeholders.
10. **Brand Strategy:**
    - **Brand Architecture:** Planning the relationship and hierarchy between different products or sub-brands within the overall brand portfolio.
    - **Brand Growth Strategies:** Identifying avenues for brand growth, such as market penetration, product development, market expansion, or diversification.
11. **Brand Monitoring and Evaluation:**
    - **Brand Audits:** Periodic assessments of the brand's health, perception, and performance.
    - **Customer Feedback:** Gathering and analyzing customer feedback to understand how the brand is perceived.
12. **Brand Evolution:**
    - **Adaptation to Change:** Evolving the brand to remain relevant in response to shifts in the market, consumer preferences, or industry trends.
    - **Rebranding:** Undertaking a strategic overhaul of

the brand's identity, positioning, or visual elements.

13. **Ethical and Social Responsibility:**
    - **Corporate Social Responsibility (CSR):** Integrating ethical practices and social responsibility into the brand's identity.
    - **Sustainability Initiatives:** Demonstrating a commitment to environmentally and socially sustainable practices.

14. **Global Branding:**
    - **Cultural Sensitivity:** Adapting branding elements to align with diverse cultural norms and values.
    - **Localization:** Customizing marketing strategies to resonate with specific regional audiences.

A successful branding strategy goes beyond visual aesthetics; it shapes the overall perception and emotional connection consumers have with a brand. Through consistent messaging, positive experiences, and a clear value proposition, brands can establish themselves in the minds of consumers, fostering loyalty and advocacy.

Chapter 6

Digital Media

Digital media refers to electronic content and communication channels that utilize digital technologies for the creation, distribution, and consumption of information. It encompasses a wide range of formats and platforms, offering various ways for people to engage with content, communicate, and share information. Here are key components and aspects of digital media:

1. **Types of Digital Media:**
    - **Text:** Digital articles, blogs, e-books, and other written content.
    - **Images:** Photographs, illustrations, infographics, and other visual content.
    - **Audio:** Podcasts, music streaming, and other forms of digital audio content.
    - **Video:** Streaming videos, vlogs, webinars, and other visual storytelling formats.
2. **Digital Platforms:**
    - **Social Media:** Platforms like Facebook, Twitter, Instagram, LinkedIn, and others for social networking and content sharing.
    - **Websites and Blogs:** Online platforms where content is published and shared.
    - **Streaming Services:** Platforms for on-demand video and audio streaming, such as YouTube, Netflix, Spotify, and others.
    - **Podcasting Platforms:** Platforms for distributing and consuming digital audio content.
3. **Interactive Media:**

- **Games and Gamification:** Interactive digital experiences, including video games and gamified applications.
- **Interactive Websites:** Websites with features like quizzes, polls, and user-generated content.

4. **Digital Advertising:**
   - **Display Ads:** Banner ads, pop-ups, and other visual advertisements on websites and apps.
   - **Social Media Ads:** Paid advertising on social media platforms.
   - **Search Engine Marketing (SEM):** Paid ads on search engine results pages.
   - **Video Ads:** Advertising within digital video content.

5. **Mobile Apps:**
   - **Mobile Applications:** Software designed for smartphones and tablets, offering various functionalities, entertainment, or services.

6. **E-commerce Platforms:**
   - **Online Marketplaces:** Platforms for buying and selling products and services online, such as Amazon, eBay, and others.
   - **E-commerce Websites:** Websites for online retail and direct-to-consumer sales.

7. **Communication Tools:**
   - **Email:** Digital communication through electronic mail.
   - **Instant Messaging:** Real-time text-based communication through platforms like WhatsApp, Messenger, and others.
   - **Video Conferencing:** Platforms like Zoom,

Microsoft Teams, and Skype for virtual face-to-face communication.
8. **Content Management Systems (CMS):**
    - **Website Builders:** Platforms like WordPress, Wix, and Squarespace for creating and managing digital content.
    - **Enterprise CMS:** Systems for organizing and managing large-scale digital content for businesses and organizations.
9. **Digital Publishing:**
    - **E-books:** Digital books available in electronic format.
    - **Online Magazines and Newspapers:** Digital versions of traditional print publications.
10. **Virtual and Augmented Reality (VR/AR):**
    - **Virtual Reality:** Immersive digital experiences that simulate real-world environments.
    - **Augmented Reality:** Overlaying digital content onto the real world, often through smartphone apps or AR glasses.
11. **Digital Analytics:**
    - **Web Analytics:** Tools for measuring and analyzing website traffic, user behavior, and engagement.
    - **Social Media Analytics:** Tracking and analyzing performance metrics on social media platforms.
12. **Data Security and Privacy:**
    - **Encryption:** Protecting digital information through encryption technologies.
    - **Privacy Policies:** Establishing guidelines and practices to protect user privacy.

13. **Digital Trends:**
    - **Artificial Intelligence (AI):** Integration of AI technologies for personalization, automation, and data analysis.
    - **Voice Search:** Growing use of voice-activated search through devices like smart speakers and voice assistants.
    - **Live Streaming:** Real-time broadcasting of video content over the internet.
14. **Digital Literacy:**
    - **Education and Training:** Initiatives to enhance individuals' skills and knowledge in using digital technologies effectively.
    - **Cybersecurity Awareness:** Promoting awareness of online security risks and best practices.

Digital media has transformed how information is created, consumed, and shared, offering new opportunities for communication, entertainment, and business. It continues to evolve with advancements in technology, shaping the way people interact in the digital age.

Social Media

Social media refers to online platforms and websites that facilitate the creation, sharing, and exchange of user-generated content, as well as the networking and interaction among users. Social media plays a significant role in connecting people, fostering communities, and facilitating communication in various forms. Here are key components and aspects of social media:

1. **Social Networking Platforms:**
    - **Facebook:** A general-purpose social networking site that allows users to connect with friends, share updates, and join groups.
    - **Twitter:** A microblogging platform where users share short messages called tweets.
    - **Instagram:** A visual-centric platform for sharing photos and videos.
    - **LinkedIn** A professional networking platform for business and career-related connections.
    - **Pinterest:** A platform for discovering and saving visual content like images and infographics.
    - **Snapchat:** A multimedia messaging app for sharing photos and videos that disappear after a short time.
    - **TikTok:** A short-form video platform for creating and sharing user-generated content.
2. **Content Sharing and Creation:**
    - **Text Posts:** Sharing written updates, thoughts, or messages.
    - **Images and Graphics:** Posting photos, graphics, and visual content.

- **Videos:** Sharing short or long-form videos on various topics.
- **Live Streaming:** Broadcasting live video content in real-time.
- **User-Generated Content (UGC):** Content created by users, often shared and reposted by others.

3. **Social Media Messaging:**
   - **Private Messaging:** Sending direct messages to individuals or groups.
   - **Group Chats:** Communicating with multiple people in a single chat.
   - **Stickers and Emojis:** Adding visual elements to express emotions in messages.

4. **Social Media Marketing:**
   - **Paid Advertising:** Promoting products or services through paid campaigns on social media platforms.
   - **Influencer Marketing:** Collaborating with influencers to promote brands or products.
   - **Content Marketing:** Creating and sharing valuable content to attract and engage audiences.

5. **Engagement and Interactions:**
   - **Likes:** Expressing approval or acknowledgment of posts.
   - **Comments:** Providing feedback or engaging in discussions on posts.
   - **Shares/Retweets:** Reposting content to one's network.
   - **Followers/Friends:** Building a network of connections with other users.

6. **Privacy and Security:**

- **Privacy Settings:** Customizing the visibility of personal information and posts.
- **Two-factor authentication:** Adding an extra layer of security to accounts.
- **Reporting and Blocking:** Tools to report inappropriate content and block users.

7. **Analytics and Insights:**
   - **Platform Analytics:** Providing data on post-performance, audience demographics, and engagement.
   - **Third-Party Tools:** Utilizing external tools for in-depth social media analytics.

8. **Trends and Hashtags:**
   - **Hashtags:** Using keywords or phrases preceded by the '#' symbol to categorize and discover content.
   - **Trending Topics:** Popular and widely discussed topics on social media.

9. **Community Building:**
   - **Groups and Communities:** Joining or creating communities based on shared interests or goals.
   - **Events:** Creating or participating in online events and gatherings.

10. **Social Listening:**
    - **Monitoring Mentions:** Tracking brand mentions and conversations about specific topics.
    - **Sentiment Analysis:** Analyzing the sentiment (positive, negative, or neutral) of social media mentions.

11. **Crisis Management:**
    - **Responding to Issues:** Addressing and managing

public relations challenges on social media.
- **Apologizing and Correcting:** Taking corrective actions and communicating transparently during crises.

12. **Educational and Informational Content:**
    - **News and Updates:** Sharing current events and news articles.
    - **Educational Content:** Providing informative and instructional materials.

Social media has become an integral part of modern communication, influencing how individuals, businesses, and organizations connect with their audiences. It continues to evolve, introducing new features, trends, and challenges, and remains a dynamic platform for expression, engagement, and community-building.

Online Journalism

Online journalism, also known as digital journalism or web journalism, refers to the production and distribution of news content through online platforms and digital technologies. As the internet has become a primary source of news consumption, online journalism has evolved to encompass a wide range of formats, styles, and delivery methods. Here are key aspects and considerations related to online journalism:

1. **Digital Platforms:**
    - **News Websites:** Dedicated online platforms for news organizations to publish articles, multimedia content, and updates.
    - **Blogs:** Personal or organizational blogs that cover news and analysis.
    - **Social Media:** Distribution of news through platforms like Twitter, Facebook, and Instagram.
    - **News Aggregators:** Platforms that compile and curate news content from various sources.
2. **Multimedia Content:**
    - **Text Articles:** Traditional written articles covering news, features, analyses, and opinion pieces.
    - **Photos and Infographics:** Visual elements to enhance storytelling and provide context.
    - **Videos:** Video reports, interviews, and documentaries.
    - **Podcasts:** Audio content featuring news discussions, interviews, and storytelling.
3. **Real-Time Updates:**
    - **Live Blogging:** Continuous updates on unfolding

events in real-time.
- **Breaking News Alerts:** Instant notifications for significant news developments.

4. **Audience Interaction:**
   - **Comments and Feedback:** Allowing readers to comment on articles and engage in discussions.
   - **Social Media Engagement:** Encouraging readers to share, like, and comment on news stories.

5. **Hyperlinking and Citations:**
   - **Hyperlinks:** Referencing and linking to external sources for additional context and verification.
   - **Attribution:** Citing sources to maintain transparency and credibility.

6. **Data Journalism:**
   - **Data Visualization:** Using charts, graphs, and interactive tools to present complex information.
   - **Investigative Data Reporting:** Analyzing large datasets to uncover insights and trends.

7. **Search Engine Optimization (SEO):**
   - **Optimizing Content:** Enhancing online visibility through keyword optimization and other SEO strategies.
   - **Headline Writing:** Crafting headlines that are both compelling and search-friendly.

8. **Mobile Journalism (MoJo):**
   - **Mobile Reporting:** Using smartphones for capturing, editing, and sharing news content.
   - **Social Media Reporting:** Reporting directly from the field through social media platforms.

9. **Digital Storytelling:**

- **Interactive Features:** Including interactive maps, timelines, and multimedia elements.
- **Long-Form Narratives:** In-depth storytelling that goes beyond traditional article formats.

10. **Monetization Models:**
    - **Subscription Models:** Offering premium content to paid subscribers.
    - **Advertising:** Generating revenue through display ads, sponsored content, and native advertising.
    - **Donations and Memberships:** Seeking financial support from readers.

11. **Ethical Considerations:**
    - **Fact-checking:** Verifying information before publishing to maintain accuracy.
    - **Transparency:** Disclosing conflicts of interest and the editorial process.
    - **Responsible Social Media Use:** Avoiding the spread of misinformation and sensationalism.

12. **Adaptation to Emerging Technologies:**
    - **Virtual Reality (VR) and Augmented Reality (AR):** Exploring immersive storytelling experiences.
    - **Artificial Intelligence (AI):** Using AI for content recommendations and data analysis.

13. **Challenges in Online Journalism:**
    - **Misinformation and Fake News:** Addressing the spread of false or misleading information.
    - **Monetization Struggles:** Navigating revenue challenges in the digital landscape.
    - **Digital Security:** Protecting journalists and sources in the online environment.

Online journalism continues to shape the media landscape, offering immediacy, interactivity, and a global reach. It requires journalists to adapt to evolving technologies, maintain ethical standards, and engage with audiences in new and innovative ways. The digital era has transformed not only how news is delivered but also the relationship between journalists and their readers.

Blogging and Content Creation

Blogging and content creation involve the development and publication of written, visual, or multimedia content on online platforms. Blogs serve as a medium for individuals, businesses, and organizations to share information, insights, and stories with their target audiences. Content creation, on the other hand, encompasses a broader range of materials produced for various purposes, including blog posts, articles, videos, infographics, and more. Here are key considerations and practices related to blogging and content creation:

Blogging:

1. **Platform Selection:**
   - **Self-Hosted Blogs:** Using platforms like WordPress.org for full control over the blog and its customization.
   - **Hosted Platforms:** Utilizing platforms like WordPress.com, Blogger, or Medium for simplified hosting.
2. **Niche and Audience:**
   - **Identifying a Niche:** Focusing on a specific topic or industry to attract a targeted audience.
   - **Understanding the Audience:** Knowing the preferences and interests of the target audience.
3. **Content Planning:**
   - **Editorial Calendar:** Planning and organizing content creation with a schedule.
   - **Content Pillars:** Identifying core topics or themes that align with the blog's focus.
4. **Writing Style:**
   - **Conversational Tone:** Adopting a friendly and

approachable writing style.
- **Clarity and Conciseness:** Ensuring content is easy to read and understand.

5. **Visual Elements:**
   - **Images and Graphics:** Incorporating visuals to enhance the appeal of blog posts.
   - **Infographics:** Presenting information in a visually engaging format.

6. **Engagement and Interaction:**
   - **Comments Section:** Encouraging readers to leave comments and engage in discussions.
   - **Social Media Integration:** Sharing blog posts on social media platforms for increased visibility.

7. **Search Engine Optimization (SEO):**
   - **Keyword Research:** Identifying relevant keywords for improved search engine rankings.
   - **Meta Tags:** Optimizing title tags, meta descriptions, and image alt text.

8. **Monetization:**
   - **Affiliate Marketing:** Promoting products or services and earning a commission for sales.
   - **Ad Revenue:** Displaying ads on the blog for income.
   - **Sponsored Content:** Collaborating with brands for sponsored posts.

9. **Consistency:**
   - **Regular Posting:** Maintaining a consistent posting schedule to keep the audience engaged.
   - **Quality Over Quantity:** Prioritizing quality content over frequent but less valuable posts.

10. **Networking:**

- **Building Relationships:** Connecting with other bloggers and influencers in the niche.
- **Guest Posting:** Writing and publishing posts on other relevant blogs for exposure.

11. **Analytics and Metrics:**
    - **Traffic Analysis:** Using tools like Google Analytics to monitor website traffic.
    - **Audience Insights:** Understanding reader demographics and behavior.

Content Creation (Beyond Blogging):

1. **Diverse Formats:**
   - **Written Content:** Articles, blog posts, e-books, and whitepapers.
   - **Visual Content:** Infographics, images, and presentations.
   - **Video Content:** Tutorials, vlogs, and webinars.
   - **Audio Content:** Podcasts and audio recordings.
2. **Storytelling:**
   - **Narrative Structure:** Weaving stories to engage and captivate the audience.
   - **Human Connection:** Creating content that resonates emotionally with the audience.
3. **Content Promotion:**
   - **Social Media Marketing:** Sharing content on platforms like Facebook, Twitter, and LinkedIn.
   - **Email Marketing:** Utilizing newsletters to distribute content to subscribers.
   - **Influencer Collaborations:** Partnering with influencers to expand reach.

4. **Evergreen and Timely Content:**
    - **Evergreen Content:** Timeless and relevant content that remains valuable over an extended period.
    - **Timely Content:** Addressing current trends, events, and industry news.
5. **Content Repurposing:**
    - **Updating and Refreshing:** Keeping older content relevant through updates.
    - **Repurposing Across Formats:** Turning written content into videos, infographics, or vice versa.
6. **User-Generated Content (UGC):**
    - **Contests and Challenges:** Encouraging users to create and share content related to the brand or topic.
    - **Testimonials and Reviews:** Showcasing user feedback and experiences.
7. **Brand Voice and Consistency:**
    - **Consistent Tone:** Maintaining a uniform brand voice across all content.
    - **Brand Guidelines:** Establishing rules for content creation to align with the brand identity.
8. **Educational and Informative Content:**
    - **Tutorials and How-Tos:** Providing step-by-step guides and instructional content.
    - **Research and Insights:** Sharing industry insights, trends, and analyses.
9. **Accessibility and Inclusivity:**
    - **Accessible Design:** Ensuring content is accessible to individuals with disabilities.
    - **Inclusive Language:** Using language that is

respectful and inclusive of diverse audiences.
10. **Feedback and Iteration:**
    - **User Feedback:** Listening to audience feedback and making improvements.
    - **Performance Analytics:** Analyzing content metrics and adjusting strategies accordingly.

Both blogging and content creation are dynamic processes that require adaptability and creativity. Consistently delivering valuable and engaging content tailored to the target audience helps build a loyal readership or audience over time.

Multimedia Storytelling

Multimedia storytelling involves the use of various media formats, such as text, images, audio, video, and interactive elements, to convey a narrative or story. This approach leverages different communication channels to create a richer and more engaging storytelling experience. Here are key components and considerations in multimedia storytelling:

1. **Story Development:**
    - **Narrative Structure:** Craft a compelling storyline with a clear beginning, middle, and end.
    - **Character Development:** Create relatable characters that resonate with the audience.
    - **Themes and Messages:** Identify the central themes and messages to be communicated.
2. **Media Integration:**
    - **Textual Content:** Use written content to provide context, details, and background information.
    - **Images and Graphics:** Enhance storytelling with visuals, including photographs, illustrations, and infographics.
    - **Audio Elements:** Incorporate background music, sound effects, and voiceovers to evoke emotions.
    - **Video Components:** Integrate video clips, interviews, and visual storytelling for a dynamic experience.
    - **Interactive Elements:** Implement features like clickable elements, quizzes, or user-driven navigation.

UNDERSTANDING MASS COMMUNICATION IN THE DIGITAL AGE

3. **Platform Considerations:**
   - **Responsive Design:** Ensure that multimedia elements are accessible and display well across different devices.
   - **Social Media Integration:** Optimize content for sharing on social platforms and leverage their features for engagement.
   - **Cross-Platform Compatibility:** Create content that can be shared and experienced seamlessly across various online platforms.

4. **User Engagement:**
   - **Interactive Storytelling:** Allow users to participate in the story through choices or interactive features.
   - **Comments and Feedback:** Encourage audience interaction by providing a space for comments and feedback.
   - **Social Sharing:** Integrate easy sharing options to facilitate the spread of the multimedia story.

5. **Visual Storytelling Techniques:**
   - **Photo Essays:** Convey a story primarily through a series of photographs.
   - **Infographics:** Use visual representations of information to enhance understanding.
   - **Comics and Graphic Novels:** Combine visuals and text to tell a story in a sequential format.
   - **Motion Graphics:** Use animated graphics and text to add movement and visual interest.

6. **Audio Storytelling:**
   - **Podcasts:** Share stories through audio-only formats, featuring narration, interviews, and soundscapes.

- **Soundscapes:** Use ambient sounds and audio effects to create a specific atmosphere.
- **Voice Narration:** Engage the audience with a compelling voiceover to guide the narrative.

7. **Video Storytelling:**
   - **Documentaries:** Create in-depth video narratives that explore real-life events or subjects.
   - **Interviews:** Use video interviews to capture personal stories and perspectives.
   - **Short Films:** Develop concise and impactful narratives through short video formats.

8. **Virtual and Augmented Reality (VR/AR):**
   - **Virtual Reality:** Immerse users in a 360-degree environment for an interactive and immersive experience.
   - **Augmented Reality:** Overlay digital elements into the real world, enhancing the user's perception.

9. **Data-Driven Storytelling:**
   - **Data Visualizations:** Use charts, graphs, and interactive data displays to tell stories with statistical information.
   - **Interactive Maps:** Present geographic data in an engaging and informative way.

10. **Cross-Media Storytelling:**
    - **Transmedia Narratives:** Extend the story across multiple platforms and media formats for a cohesive experience.
    - **Integrated Campaigns:** Combine traditional media, digital platforms, and experiential elements to tell a unified story.

11. **Emotional Resonance:**
    - **Music and Soundtrack:** Utilize music to enhance emotional impact and create a memorable atmosphere.
    - **Emotive Visuals:** Choose visuals that evoke specific emotions and enhance the overall storytelling experience.
12. **Accessibility:**
    - **Closed Captions:** Provide text captions for video and audio content to make it accessible to a broader audience.
    - **Alt Text for Images:** Include descriptive alternative text for images to assist those with visual impairments.

Multimedia storytelling offers a dynamic and immersive way to connect with audiences, allowing them to engage with content on multiple levels. Whether through a combination of text, images, audio, or video, the goal is to create a cohesive and impactful narrative that resonates with the audience.

Chapter 7

Media Theory

Media theory refers to the academic study and analysis of media, communication, and their effects on society. It encompasses a wide range of perspectives and approaches that seek to understand the role, impact, and dynamics of media in shaping human communication and culture. Media theories provide frameworks for examining how media messages are produced, distributed, received, and interpreted. Here are some key media theories:

1. **Mass Communication Theory:**
    - **Hypodermic Needle Theory (Magic Bullet Theory):** Suggests that media messages are like a "magic bullet" that directly influences and shapes the opinions and behaviors of the audience.
    - **Two-Step Flow Theory:** Proposes that media messages are first received by opinion leaders who then influence others in a two-step process.
2. **Communication Models:**
    - **Shannon-Weaver Model:** Describes communication as a linear process involving a sender, a message, a channel, a receiver, and feedback.
    - **Transactional Model:** Emphasizes the dynamic and interactive nature of communication, with both sender and receiver playing active roles.
3. **Cultural Studies:**
    - **Encoding-Decoding Model:** Developed by Stuart Hall, this model explores how media producers encode messages and how audiences decode and interpret them based on their cultural contexts and experiences.
4. **Agenda-Setting Theory:**

- **McCombs and Shaw's Agenda-Setting:** Proposes that media has the power to influence public perception by highlighting certain issues, leading the audience to perceive them as more important.

5. **Cultural Imperialism:**
   - **Media Dependency Theory:** Suggests that individuals and societies become dependent on media for information and that media has the power to influence public opinion and shape cultural values.

6. **Cultural Effects Theories:**
   - **Cultivation Theory:** Developed by George Gerbner, this theory explores the long-term effects of television viewing on shaping individuals' perceptions of reality.
   - **Media Ecology Theory:** Coined by Marshall McLuhan, this theory examines how media and communication technologies shape human environments and cultures.

7. **Political Economy of Media:**
   - **Critical Political Economy:** Focuses on the economic and political structures that influence media ownership, content production, and distribution.

8. **Framing Theory:**
   - **Framing Analysis:** Explores how media frames news stories by emphasizing certain aspects while downplaying others, shaping public perception.

9. **Uses and Gratifications:**
   - **Audience-Centered Approach:** Examines why and how audiences use media to fulfill certain needs, such as information, entertainment, or social connection.

10. **Technological Determinism:**
    - **McLuhan's Medium is the Message:** Argues that the medium through which information is conveyed has a more significant impact on society than the actual content.

11. **Reception Theory:**
    - **Stuart Hall's Reception Theory:** Focuses on how audiences actively interpret and make meaning from media texts, emphasizing the role of the audience in shaping the message.

12. **Postmodern Media Theory:**
     - **Jean Baudrillard's Simulacra and Simulation:** Explores the idea that in a postmodern society, reality is replaced by simulations and signs, challenging traditional notions of truth.
13. **Network Society Theory:**
     - **Manuel Castells' Network Society:** Examines the impact of digital communication technologies on society, emphasizing the role of networks in shaping social structures and interactions.
14. **Surveillance Studies:**
     - **Foucault's Panopticon:** Describes a society where surveillance becomes a mechanism of social control, influencing behavior through the perception of being watched.
15. **Postcolonial Media Theory:**
     - **Edward Said's Orientalism:** Explores how media representations contribute to the construction of stereotypes and power imbalances between Western and non-Western cultures.

These theories provide frameworks for understanding the complex and multifaceted relationships between media, communication, and society. Scholars and researchers continue to build upon and critique these theories in response to the evolving landscape of media and technology

Communication Theories

Communication theories are frameworks that seek to understand and explain the processes, dynamics, and effects of communication in various contexts. These theories cover a wide range of perspectives, from interpersonal communication to mass communication, and they contribute to our understanding of how messages are created, transmitted, received, and interpreted. Here are some key communication theories:

1. **Communication Models:**
    - **Shannon-Weaver Model:** Describes communication as a linear process involving a sender, a message, a channel, a receiver, and feedback.
    - **Transactional Model:** Emphasizes the dynamic and interactive nature of communication, with both sender and receiver playing active roles.
2. **Interpersonal Communication Theories:**
    - **Social Penetration Theory:** Explores how relationships develop through self-disclosure and increased intimacy.
    - **Social Exchange Theory:** Examines communication in terms of the costs and rewards associated with interpersonal interactions.
    - **Relational Dialectics Theory:** Explores the tensions and contradictions inherent in close relationships.
3. **Group and Organizational Communication:**
    - **Groupthink Theory:** Discusses the negative

consequences of group consensus and the suppression of dissenting opinions.
- **Organizational Culture Theory:** Examines how communication shapes and is shaped by the culture of an organization.

4. **Media and Mass Communication Theories:**
   - **Agenda-Setting Theory:** Proposes that media influences public perception by highlighting certain issues.
   - **Cultivation Theory:** Explores the long-term effects of television viewing on shaping individuals' perceptions of reality.
   - **Uses and Gratifications:** Examines why and how audiences use media to fulfill certain needs.

5. **Rhetorical and Persuasion Theories:**
   - **Elaboration Likelihood Model (ELM):** Describes the two routes to persuasion—central (logical) and peripheral (emotional).
   - **Aristotle's Rhetorical Triangle:** Emphasizes the interplay between the speaker, the audience, and the message in persuasive communication.

6. **Semiotics and Symbolic Interactionism:**
   - **Symbolic Interactionism:** Explores how symbols and language shape human interaction and the construction of meaning.
   - **Semiotics:** Studies signs, symbols, and their interpretations as a means of communication.

7. **Communication Accommodation Theory:**
   - **Convergence and Divergence:** Examines how individuals adjust their communication styles to either match or differ from others in social interactions.

8. **Diffusion of Innovations:**
   - **Rogers' Diffusion of Innovations:** Describes the process by which new ideas or innovations spread through a society or social system.

9. **Cognitive Dissonance Theory:**
   - **Leon Festinger's Theory:** Explores the discomfort individuals feel when holding conflicting beliefs, leading to a desire for consistency.

10. **Uncertainty Reduction Theory:**
    - **Charles Berger's Theory:** Examines how communication can reduce uncertainty in initial interactions between people.

11. **Communication Privacy Management Theory:**
    - **Sandra Petronio's Theory:** Explores how individuals manage their private information in interpersonal relationships.

12. **Communication and Culture:**
    - **Edward T. Hall's High and Low Context Cultures:** Examines the role of context in communication and how it varies across different cultures.

13. **Narrative Paradigm:**
    - **Walter Fisher's Theory:** Posits that humans are inherently storytellers and that people make decisions based on persuasive stories.

14. **Face-Negotiation Theory:**
    - **Stella Ting-Toomey's Theory:** Examines how individuals from different cultures manage face, or self-image, in communication.

15. **Media Ecology Theory:**
    - **Marshall McLuhan's Theory:** Explores how media and communication technologies shape human environments and cultures.

These theories provide frameworks for analyzing and understanding communication processes, behaviors, and outcomes in diverse settings. Communication scholars often draw upon multiple theories to gain a comprehensive understanding of the complexities inherent in human communication.

Cultural Studies

Cultural Studies is an interdisciplinary field of academic study that explores the complex interplay between culture, society, and power. It emerged in the mid-20th century and has since evolved, incorporating perspectives from sociology, anthropology, literature, media studies, and other disciplines. Cultural Studies seeks to understand how culture influences and is influenced by various social, political, economic, and historical factors. Here are key aspects and concepts related to Cultural Studies:

1. **Cultural Criticism:**
   - Cultural Studies involves critical analysis and critique of cultural practices, representations, and ideologies.
   - It examines how power structures shape and are shaped by cultural phenomena.
2. **Hegemony and Power Relations:**
   - Cultural Studies draws heavily from Antonio Gramsci's concept of hegemony, which refers to the dominance of one social group over others through consent rather than force.
   - It explores how power relations are enacted and maintained through cultural practices, discourses, and institutions.
3. **Representation and Identity:**
   - Cultural Studies analyzes how various groups are represented in cultural texts, media, and discourse.
   - It explores how identity is constructed and negotiated within cultural contexts.
4. **Popular Culture:**
   - Cultural Studies places a strong emphasis on the

study of popular culture, including mass media, entertainment, fashion, and everyday practices.
- It challenges the distinctions between high culture and popular culture.

5. **Cultural Production and Consumption:**
    - Cultural Studies examines the processes of cultural production, including the creation of literature, art, media, and other forms of expression.
    - It analyzes how cultural products are consumed and interpreted by audiences.

6. **Subcultures and Counter-Cultures:**
    - Cultural Studies explores subcultures and counter-cultures as alternative expressions of identity and resistance to mainstream culture.
    - It investigates how marginalized groups develop their cultural practices and meanings.

7. **Globalization and Cultural Flows:**
    - Cultural Studies addresses the impact of globalization on cultural exchange, hybridity, and the flow of ideas, products, and practices across borders.
    - It examines the tensions between local and global cultural dynamics.

8. **Cultural Identity and Politics:**
    - Cultural Studies analyzes how cultural identity intersects with political struggles and movements.
    - It explores issues of race, gender, sexuality, class, and other identity markers in cultural contexts.

9. **Postcolonialism and Cultural Studies:**
    - Cultural Studies engages with postcolonial theory to understand the legacies of colonialism and imperialism on culture.

- It explores how cultures resist and negotiate the effects of colonial histories.
10. **Cultural Texts and Artifacts:**
    - Cultural Studies considers a wide range of cultural texts, including literature, film, music, art, advertisements, and digital media.
    - It examines how these texts communicate meaning and contribute to cultural understanding.
11. **Cultural Hegemony and Media Studies:**
    - Cultural Studies within media studies critically analyzes the role of media in shaping cultural norms, ideologies, and representations.
    - It investigates the media's influence on public opinion and identity formation.
12. **Cultural Pedagogy:**
    - Cultural Studies addresses the role of education in shaping cultural knowledge and ideologies.
    - It explores how educational institutions contribute to the reproduction of cultural values.
13. **Everyday Life Studies:**
    - Cultural Studies examines the routines, rituals, and practices of everyday life.
    - It considers how everyday activities contribute to the reproduction or transformation of culture.
14. **Cultural Capital and Bourdieu:**
    - Cultural Studies engages with Pierre Bourdieu's concept of cultural capital, which refers to the symbolic resources individuals possess and use for social mobility.
    - It explores how cultural practices contribute to social distinctions.

Cultural Studies is characterized by its commitment to interdisciplinary and critical approaches, emphasizing the importance of understanding culture as a dynamic and contested terrain. Scholars in Cultural Studies often draw from a variety of theoretical frameworks to analyze and interpret cultural phenomena in their social and historical contexts.

Semiotics

Semiotics, often referred to as the study of signs and symbols, is a field of study that explores how signs and symbols convey meaning within different contexts. Developed in the late 19th and early 20th centuries by scholars such as Ferdinand de Saussure and Charles Sanders Peirce, semiotics provides a framework for analyzing how signs function as carriers of meaning in various forms of communication, including language, visual arts, literature, and everyday life. Here are key concepts and aspects related to semiotics:

1. **Signs and Signifiers:**
   - **Sign:** In semiotics, a sign is composed of two parts—the signifier (the form in which the sign is expressed, such as a word or an image) and the signified (the concept or meaning associated with the sign).
2. **Semiotic Elements:**
   - **Icon:** A sign that resembles or imitates the thing it signifies (e.g., a picture of a tree).
   - **Index:** A sign that is directly connected or associated with its referent through causality or correlation (e.g., smoke as an index of fire).
   - **Symbol:** A sign that conveys meaning through cultural convention or agreement (e.g., a national flag).
3. **Syntagmatic and Paradigmatic Relations:**
   - **Syntagmatic Relations:** The way signs are combined or sequenced in a particular order (e.g., words in a sentence).
   - **Paradigmatic Relations:** The selection of one sign over others in a particular context (e.g., choosing a specific word to convey a particular meaning).

4. **Semiotic Analysis:**
    - **Denotation:** The literal or primary meaning of a sign, often associated with its dictionary definition.
    - **Connotation:** The secondary, cultural, or subjective meanings that a sign carries beyond its denotation.
5. **Semiotic Modes:**
    - **Verbal Semiotics:** The study of signs in language, including the analysis of words, phrases, and syntax.
    - **Visual Semiotics:** The study of signs in visual representations, such as images, paintings, and symbols.
6. **Semiotics in Linguistics:**
    - **Ferdinand de Saussure:** Considered the founder of modern linguistics, Saussure's work emphasized the study of language as a system of signs and introduced the concepts of langue (language system) and parole (individual speech acts).
7. **Peircean Semiotics:**
    - **Charles Sanders Peirce:** Introduced a broader understanding of signs, categorizing them into icons, indexes, and symbols. Peirce's triadic model also includes the concepts of Firstness, Secondness, and Thirdness, which represent different aspects of sign interpretation.
8. **Semiotics in Visual Arts:**
    - **Roland Barthes:** Applied semiotics to the analysis of visual and cultural phenomena, including photography and advertising, in works like "Mythologies" and "Image-Music-Text."
9. **Cultural Semiotics:**
    - **Umberto Eco:** Expanded semiotics to the study of culture and communication, examining how signs operate within cultural systems. His work "A Theory of Semiotics" explores various aspects of signification.
10. **Applied Semiotics:**
    - **Advertising Semiotics:** Analyzing the use of signs and symbols in advertising to convey specific

meanings and influence consumer behavior.
- **Film Semiotics:** Examining how signs and symbols contribute to meaning in films, including the study of cinematography, mise-en-scène, and editing.

11. **Semiotics in Everyday Life:**
    - **Fashion Semiotics:** Exploring how clothing and fashion choices function as signs that communicate identity, status, and cultural affiliations.
    - **Urban Semiotics:** Analyzing the signs and symbols present in the urban environment, including signage, architecture, and street art.

12. **Critical Semiotics:**
    - **Deconstruction:** A critical approach that questions and challenges the stability of meanings in signs, emphasizing the ambiguity and fluidity of interpretations.
    - **Postmodern Semiotics:** Examining how signs and symbols operate in a postmodern context characterized by pluralism, fragmentation, and intertextuality.

Semiotics provides a versatile framework for understanding how signs and symbols structure our perception of the world and influence communication. It is applied across various disciplines to analyze and interpret meaning in diverse cultural, linguistic, and visual contexts.

Media Ecology

Media ecology is a theoretical framework that examines the relationship between media, technology, communication, and the human environment. Developed by Marshall McLuhan in the 1960s and further expanded upon by other scholars, media ecology explores how different communication technologies shape and influence human perception, cognition, and social structures. The concept emphasizes the interconnectedness of media and their impact on the ecology of human experience. Here are key aspects and concepts related to media ecology:

1. **Tetrad of Media Effects:**
    - Developed by Marshall McLuhan, the tetrad consists of four questions to analyze the effects of media on human culture:
        - **What does the medium enhance or amplify?**
        - **What does the medium obsolesce or push aside?**
        - **What does the medium retrieve or bring back from the past?**
        - **What does the medium reverse or flip into when pushed to its limits?**
2. **The Medium is the Message:**
    - One of McLuhan's most famous statements, this concept suggests that the medium through which information is transmitted is as influential as the content itself. The medium shapes how the message is perceived and understood.
3. **Global Village:**
    - McLuhan introduced the idea of a "global village," suggesting that electronic media, particularly

television, would create a sense of interconnectedness, making the world akin to a small village where information and communication are instantaneously shared.

4. **Hot and Cool Media:**
   - McLuhan classified media into "hot" and "cool" categories. Hot media are high in definition and require less audience involvement (e.g., radio), while cool media are low in definition and demand more participation (e.g., television).

5. **Technological Determinism:**
   - Media ecology incorporates elements of technological determinism, the belief that technology shapes and drives social and cultural change. It suggests that the characteristics of communication technologies influence the way people think, perceive, and interact.

6. **Media Literacy:**
   - Media ecology encourages media literacy by prompting individuals to critically examine the effects of media on their lives, culture, and society. It emphasizes the importance of understanding how media shape perceptions and influence behavior.

7. **Media Environments:**
   - The concept of media environments refers to the overall context and conditions created by different media technologies. It considers how media environments influence individuals and societies on a large scale.

8. **Orality and Literacy:**
   - Media ecology explores the transition from oral cultures to literate cultures and, more recently, to

electronic and digital cultures. Each shift in communication technologies has profound effects on cognition, memory, and social organization.
9. **Biological and Psychic Effects:**
    ○ Media ecology examines the biological and psychological impacts of media on individuals. It considers how media technologies influence sensory perception, attention spans, and cognitive processes.
10. **Extensions of Man:**
    ○ McLuhan referred to media as "extensions of man," emphasizing that technologies are not merely tools but integral parts of human existence that extend and shape human capabilities and experiences.
11. **Temporal Resonance:**
    ○ Neil Postman, a scholar influenced by McLuhan, introduced the concept of temporal resonance. It suggests that different media technologies influence the perception of time, shaping individuals' sense of past, present, and future.
12. **Ecological Balance and Overload:**
    ○ Media ecology raises concerns about information overload and the need for balance in media consumption. It considers how an excess of information and communication technologies may disrupt the ecological balance of human experience.

Media ecology remains a relevant and evolving field of study, particularly in the context of rapid technological advancements. Scholars continue to explore how new media technologies reshape communication patterns, social structures, and individual experiences within the broader ecological context.

Chapter 8

Media Law and Ethics

Media law and ethics are crucial components of journalism and communication, providing guidelines and standards for responsible and accountable media practices. These areas of study help ensure that media professionals uphold principles of truth, accuracy, fairness, and transparency while respecting legal boundaries. Here are key aspects of media law and ethics:

Media Law:

1. **Freedom of Speech and Press Freedom:**
     - Protection of the right to freedom of speech and the press is a fundamental aspect of media law, varying across legal systems and jurisdictions.
     - Legal frameworks aim to balance freedom of expression with the protection of individuals and public interests.
2. **Libel and Defamation:**
     - Laws govern statements that harm an individual's reputation (defamation). Journalists must be cautious to avoid making false statements that damage someone's character.
3. **Privacy Laws:**
     - Privacy laws protect individuals from unwarranted intrusion into their private lives. Journalists must navigate the delicate balance between the public's right to know and an individual's right to privacy.
4. **Copyright and Intellectual Property:**
     - Media professionals must respect intellectual property rights, including copyrights, trademarks, and patents.
     - Fair use provisions and exceptions may apply,

allowing limited use of copyrighted material for purposes such as news reporting or commentary.

5. **Access to Information:**
   - Laws often govern the public's right to access government information. Journalists may use freedom of information laws to request and obtain government records.

6. **Contempt of Court:**
   - Journalists must be aware of laws regarding contempt of court, which restrict the reporting of certain details during ongoing legal proceedings to ensure a fair trial.

7. **Prior Restraint:**
   - Legal systems typically discourage prior restraint, where the government attempts to prevent media from publishing or broadcasting content before it is disseminated.

8. **Broadcasting Regulations:**
   - Broadcast media may be subject to specific regulations regarding content, licensing, and ownership to ensure fair and diverse representation.

9. **National Security Laws:**
   - Laws related to national security may restrict the publication of certain information deemed sensitive for reasons of national interest.

Media Ethics:

1. **Truth and Accuracy:**
   - Journalists are expected to report truthfully and accurately, verifying information before publishing or broadcasting it.
   - Corrections should be promptly issued for errors.

2. **Independence and Impartiality:**
   - Media professionals should maintain independence from outside influences, including advertisers, governments, and other external entities.
   - Impartiality requires presenting news and information fairly and without bias.
3. **Fairness and Objectivity:**
   - Journalists should treat all subjects with fairness and present a balanced view of events. Avoiding stereotypes and discrimination is essential.
4. **Minimizing Harm:**
   - Journalists must weigh the public's right to know against potential harm. They should minimize harm to individuals and communities while reporting important news.
5. **Privacy and Sensitivity:**
   - Respecting individuals' privacy is crucial. Journalists should exercise sensitivity, especially when reporting on tragedies, victims, and vulnerable populations.
6. **Conflicts of Interest:**
   - Media professionals should avoid conflicts of interest that could compromise their journalistic integrity. Full disclosure of potential conflicts is essential.
7. **Accountability and Corrections:**
   - Media organizations and professionals should be accountable for their work. When errors occur, corrections and clarifications should be issued promptly.
8. **Community Engagement:**
   - Engaging with the community and seeking public input can enhance media credibility and

responsiveness to audience needs.

9. **Diversity and Inclusivity:**
    - Journalists should strive for diversity and inclusivity in their coverage, ensuring a range of voices and perspectives are represented.
10. **Transparent Sourcing:**
    - attributing information to its source helps maintain transparency and enables audiences to assess the credibility of the information.

Media law and ethics work in tandem to establish a framework for responsible journalism, providing both legal boundaries and ethical guidelines to guide media professionals in their work. Adhering to these principles is essential for maintaining public trust in the media and ensuring the integrity of the information disseminated to the public.

Freedom of the Press

Freedom of the press is a fundamental principle that upholds the right of journalists and media organizations to report news and express opinions without government interference or censorship. It is a cornerstone of democratic societies and is often enshrined in national constitutions or legal frameworks. Here are key aspects and considerations related to freedom of the press:

Key Principles and Concepts:

1. **First Amendment (United States):**
    - In the United States, freedom of the press is protected by the First Amendment of the Constitution, which states, "Congress shall make no law... abridging the freedom of speech, or of the press."
2. **International Standards:**
    - The Universal Declaration of Human Rights (Article 19) and the International Covenant on Civil and Political Rights (Article 19) recognize the right to freedom of expression, which encompasses freedom of the press.
3. **Government Non-Interference:**
    - Freedom of the press prohibits government censorship or control over media content. Governments should not interfere with the gathering, reporting, or dissemination of news.
4. **Pluralism and Diversity:**
    - A free press supports pluralism and diverse voices. It allows for a variety of opinions and perspectives, contributing to a well-informed public and robust democratic discourse.

5. **Public's Right to Know:**
   - Freedom of the press is linked to the public's right to know. It enables citizens to access information about government activities, public issues, and events of significance.
6. **Investigative Journalism:**
   - Journalists are empowered to conduct investigative journalism, uncovering corruption, abuses of power, and other issues that serve the public interest.
7. **Protection of Sources:**
   - Journalists often have the right to protect their sources to encourage individuals to share information without fear of retaliation.
8. **Media Independence:**
   - Media organizations should operate independently of government and commercial interests, ensuring editorial autonomy and integrity.
9. **Legal Protections:**
   - Laws may provide legal protections for journalists, such as shield laws that prevent them from being compelled to disclose their sources in court.
10. **Access to Information:**
    - Freedom of the press is linked to the public's right to access information held by the government. Laws supporting freedom of information contribute to transparency.

Challenges and Issues:

1. **Censorship and Suppression:**
   - Governments may attempt to censor or suppress media content through legal restrictions, harassment of journalists, or other means.

2. **Media Ownership and Control:**
   - Concentration of media ownership in a few hands can lead to a lack of diversity and pluralism, limiting the range of voices and perspectives.
3. **Violence and Intimidation:**
   - Journalists may face violence, intimidation, or threats, particularly when reporting on sensitive issues or exposing corruption.
4. **Online and Digital Challenges:**
   - The digital age poses challenges, including issues of misinformation, online harassment, and the spread of disinformation.
5. **Legal Restrictions:**
   - Some countries may impose legal restrictions on the press, such as defamation laws or restrictions on reporting during sensitive times.
6. **National Security Concerns:**
   - Governments may justify restrictions on press freedom in the name of national security, leading to concerns about overreach and abuse of power.
7. **Economic Pressures:**
   - Economic pressures, including advertising dependencies, can influence editorial decisions and compromise media independence.
8. **Emergencies and Crises:**
   - During emergencies or crises, governments may impose restrictions on the press in the name of public safety, raising concerns about the balance between freedom and security.

Freedom of the press requires a commitment to protecting and upholding the principles that enable journalists to fulfill their crucial role in society. It involves a delicate balance between the right to information, individual rights, and the broader public interest in maintaining an informed and engaged citizenry. Societies and legal systems continually grapple with finding this balance while addressing evolving challenges in the media landscape.

Privacy Issues

Privacy issues have become increasingly prominent with the rapid development of technology, the growth of digital communication, and the collection and dissemination of vast amounts of personal information. These issues encompass a range of concerns related to the protection of individuals' data, autonomy, and the potential for surveillance. Here are key privacy issues:

1. Data Collection and Surveillance:

- **Mass Surveillance:** Government agencies and private entities may engage in mass surveillance, monitoring individuals' communications, activities, and movements on a large scale.
- **Smart Devices:** Internet of Things (IoT) devices, such as smart home devices, wearables, and smart appliances, often collect and transmit personal data.

2. Online Privacy:

- **Tracking and Profiling:** Websites, social media platforms, and online services may track users' online activities to create profiles for targeted advertising.
- **Cookies and Tracking Technologies:** Cookies and similar technologies can be used to track users' browsing behavior, potentially without their knowledge or consent.

3. Social Media Privacy:

- **Data Sharing:** Social media platforms may share users' personal information with third-party entities, leading to concerns about data misuse.
- **Privacy Settings:** Users may not be fully aware of or understand the privacy settings on social media platforms, exposing them to unintentional data sharing.

4. Data Breaches:

- **Unauthorized Access:** Cyberattacks and data breaches can lead to unauthorized access to personal information, exposing individuals to identity theft and other forms of cybercrime.
- **Security Vulnerabilities:** Weaknesses in security measures may expose sensitive data, compromising individuals' privacy.

Intellectual Property

Intellectual property (IP) refers to creations of the mind—innovations, inventions, literary and artistic works, designs, symbols, names, and images used in commerce. Intellectual property is protected by law through patents, copyrights, trademarks, and trade secrets, allowing creators and innovators to control the use of their creations. Here are the main types of intellectual property and key considerations:

1. Patents:

- **Definition:** A patent is a legal document that grants its holder the exclusive right to make, use, and sell an invention for a specified period (usually 20 years).
- **Requirements:** Patents are granted for new, useful, and non-obvious inventions or discoveries.
- **Examples:** Inventions in various fields, such as technology, medicine, and manufacturing, can be patented.

2. Copyright:

- **Definition:** Copyright protects original works of authorship, such as literary, artistic, and musical creations, providing the creator with the exclusive right to reproduce, distribute, and display their work.
- **Requirements:** Copyright protection is automatic upon the creation of the work; no formal registration is required.
- **Examples:** Books, music, paintings, software code, and films are common subjects of copyright.

3. Trademarks:

- **Definition:** Trademarks are distinctive signs (like logos or names) used to identify and distinguish goods or services of one business from those of others.
- **Requirements:** Trademarks must be distinctive and capable of graphical representation. Registration is not mandatory but provides additional legal benefits.
- **Examples:** Logos (Nike swoosh), brand names (Apple), and slogans ("Just Do It") are protected as trademarks.

4. Trade Secrets:

- **Definition:** Trade secrets are confidential business information, such as manufacturing processes, formulas, and customer lists, which provide a competitive advantage.
- **Protection:** Trade secrets are not registered but are protected as long as they remain confidential. Misappropriation is illegal.
- **Examples:** The Coca-Cola formula and the recipe for KFC's original fried chicken are examples of trade secrets.

5. Industrial Designs:

- **Definition:** Industrial designs protect the visual design of objects that are not purely utilitarian but have an aesthetic or ornamental aspect.
- **Protection:** Design registration grants exclusive rights to the appearance of the design for a limited period.
- **Examples:** Product designs, packaging, and the appearance of consumer goods can be protected.

6. Geographical Indications:

- **Definition:** Geographical indications identify products as originating from a specific geographic location and possessing qualities, reputation, or characteristics associated with that location.
- **Protection:** They are protected to prevent misuse and unauthorized use of the indication.
- **Examples:** Champagne (sparkling wine from the Champagne region of France), Parmigiano-Reggiano (cheese from Italy).

7. Plant Variety Protection:

- **Definition:** Plant variety protection (PVP) grants exclusive rights to the breeder of a new plant variety, allowing them to control its production, sale, and distribution.
- **Protection:** PVP is granted for a limited period, typically 20 to 25 years, depending on the type of plant.
- **Examples:** New varieties of crops, flowers, and other cultivated plants.

8. Integrated Circuit Layout Designs:

- **Definition:** This form of IP protects the layout of integrated circuits (computer chips).
- **Protection:** Registration provides exclusive rights to the layout design for a specified period.
- **Examples:** Layouts of semiconductor chips and integrated circuits.

Key Considerations:

1. **Enforcement and Infringement:**
   - Owners of intellectual property must actively enforce their rights and may take legal action against infringement.
2. **Licensing and Transfer:**
   - Owners can license their intellectual property to others for use, generating revenue. IP rights can also be bought or sold.
3. **International Protection:**
   - Intellectual property protection varies globally, and creators may need to navigate different legal systems for international coverage.
4. **Balancing Innovation and Access:**
   - Intellectual property protection aims to incentivize innovation, but there's an ongoing debate about striking a balance between protection and the public's right to access information and ideas.
5. **Public Domain:**
   - Works in the public domain are not protected by intellectual property rights and can be freely used by the public. Works may enter the public domain through the expiration of protection or intentional dedication by the creator.

Intellectual property plays a crucial role in fostering innovation, creativity, and economic development. Balancing the rights of creators with the public interest remains an important consideration in shaping intellectual property policies.

Media Regulation

Media regulation refers to the oversight and control of media activities by governmental or non-governmental entities. The purpose of regulation is often to ensure that media outlets adhere to certain standards, uphold ethical principles, and serve the public interest. The specific regulatory frameworks and mechanisms vary widely across countries, reflecting diverse legal, cultural, and political contexts. Here are key aspects of media regulation:

1. Governmental vs. Self-Regulation:

- **Governmental Regulation:** In many countries, regulatory bodies or government agencies are tasked with overseeing media activities. This may involve licensing, content restrictions, and adherence to ethical standards.
- **Self-Regulation:** Some media industries operate under self-regulatory mechanisms, where industry associations or organizations establish and enforce codes of conduct and ethical standards.

2. Content Regulation:

- **Censorship:** Some countries have censorship laws that restrict or control the dissemination of certain content deemed harmful, offensive, or against public policy.
- **Classification Systems:** Media content, especially in film and television, may be subject to classification systems that indicate the suitability of the content for different audiences.

3. Media Ownership and Plurality:

- **Ownership Restrictions:** Regulations may limit the concentration of media ownership to ensure diversity and prevent undue influence by a few entities.
- **Plurality:** Some regulatory frameworks emphasize media plurality to ensure a range of voices, perspectives, and opinions in the media landscape.

4. Licensing and Spectrum Allocation:

- **Broadcast Licensing:** Governments may require broadcasters to obtain licenses to operate, with compliance conditions related to content, advertising, and other factors.

- **Spectrum Allocation:** Regulation of radio frequency spectrum is critical for broadcasting. Authorities allocate frequencies and set technical standards to avoid interference.

5. Advertising Standards:

- **Truth in Advertising:** Regulations may require truthful and transparent advertising, preventing false or misleading claims.
- **Children's Advertising:** Special rules often govern advertising targeted at children to protect them from potentially harmful content.

6. Privacy and Data Protection:

- **Data Protection Laws:** With the digitalization of media, regulations addressing the collection, use, and protection of personal data have become important to safeguard individuals' privacy.

7. Journalistic Ethics and Standards:

- **Codes of Ethics:** Regulatory bodies or industry associations may establish codes of ethics that guide journalists and media organizations in maintaining professional standards.
- **Complaints and Redress:** Mechanisms for addressing public complaints about media content, accuracy, and ethical violations may be established.

8. Internet and Social Media Regulation:

- **Online Content:** Some countries extend regulatory frameworks to cover online content, addressing issues like hate speech, misinformation, and harmful online behavior.
- **Platform Liability:** Regulations regarding the liability of online platforms for user-generated content are debated, with some countries holding platforms accountable for content moderation.

9. Community Standards and Values:

- **Cultural Sensitivity:** Media regulations often reflect cultural values and sensitivity, aiming to protect communities from content that may be offensive or culturally inappropriate.

10. Emergency and National Security Measures:

- **Emergency Powers:** Governments may have the authority to impose restrictions on media during emergencies, emphasizing national security concerns.

- **Journalist Protection:** Regulations may include provisions for the protection of journalists covering conflict zones or dangerous situations.

11. Access to Information:

- **Freedom of Information Laws:** Some countries have laws that facilitate access to government information, promoting transparency and accountability.

12. Regulatory Challenges:

- **New Media Challenges:** The dynamic nature of the media landscape, including digital platforms and social media, poses challenges for traditional regulatory frameworks.
- **Global Internet Governance:** The global nature of the Internet raises questions about cross-border enforcement and the harmonization of regulations.

13. Public Service Broadcasting:

- **Funding and Independence:** Public service broadcasters may be subject to regulations governing their funding, ensuring independence from political interference.

Media regulation is a complex and evolving field, influenced by technological advancements, societal changes, and political considerations. Striking a balance between the need for media freedom, ethical standards, and the protection of the public interest remains a challenge for regulators worldwide.

Chapter 9

Film Studies

Film studies is an academic discipline that involves the critical analysis, interpretation, and exploration of the history, theory, and aesthetics of cinema. It encompasses a wide range of topics, including the study of individual films, filmmakers, genres, film movements, and the broader cultural and social impact of cinema. Film studies draw on elements from various fields such as art, literature, history, sociology, and philosophy to understand the art and cultural significance of filmmaking. Here are key areas covered in film studies:

1. Film History:

- **Silent Cinema:** Exploration of the early years of cinema, from the Lumière Brothers to pioneers like D.W. Griffith.
- **Golden Age of Hollywood:** Study of classical Hollywood cinema, including the studio system, genres, and iconic figures like Alfred Hitchcock.
- **New Waves:** Examination of film movements such as the French New Wave, Italian Neorealism, and German Expressionism.
- **Global Cinemas:** Analysis of film industries worldwide, including Bollywood, Chinese cinema, and Latin American cinema.

2. Film Theory:

- **Formalism:** Analyzing the formal elements of film, such as cinematography, editing, sound, and mise-en-scène.
- **Auteur Theory:** Focus on the role of the director as the primary creative force in filmmaking.
- **Genre Theory:** Examination of film genres and their conventions, transformations, and cultural significance.
- **Semiotics and Film:** Application of semiotic theories to understand the signs and symbols in cinema.
- **Feminist Film Theory:** Exploration of gender roles, representation, and feminist perspectives in film.

3. Film Analysis:

- **Scene Analysis:** In-depth examination of specific scenes to understand the use of cinematic techniques and storytelling.

- **Narrative Analysis:** Study of storytelling structures, including narrative theories and the analysis of plot, character, and theme.
- **Cinematic Language:** Exploration of the visual and auditory language of cinema, including shot composition, camera movement, and editing.

4. Cinematography and Production Design:

- **Cinematography:** Analysis of the visual elements of filmmaking, including camera work, lighting, and color.
- **Production Design:** Study of the visual and aesthetic aspects of film production, including set design and costume.

5. Sound in Film:

- **Film Soundtrack:** Examination of the role of music and sound effects in enhancing the emotional impact of films.
- **Dialogue and Sound Design:** Study of the use of dialogue and sound effects in creating aural experiences.

6. Film Genres:

- **Genre Studies:** Exploration of various film genres such as comedy, drama, horror, science fiction, and the conventions associated with each.

7. National Cinemas:

- **American Cinema:** In-depth study of Hollywood and American film history.
- **European Cinema:** Exploration of major European film movements and national cinemas.
- **Asian Cinema:** Analysis of cinema from countries such as India, China, Japan, and South Korea.

8. Documentary and Non-Fiction Film:

- **Documentary Theory:** Examination of the theory and practice of documentary filmmaking.
- **Non-Fiction Cinema:** Study of non-fiction forms in film, including essay films and experimental documentaries.

9. Film and Society:

- **Cultural Studies:** Exploration of the cultural impact of films, including their reflection on societal values, norms, and ideologies.
- **Political Economy of Film:** Analysis of the economic and political factors influencing film production, distribution, and exhibition.

10. Film and Technology:

- **Digital Cinema:** Examination of the impact of digital technology on filmmaking, distribution, and exhibition.
- **Special Effects:** Study of the use of visual and practical effects in cinema.

11. Film Festivals and Reception:

- **Film Festivals:** Exploration of the role of film festivals in showcasing and promoting films.
- **Audience Reception:** Study of how audiences engage with and interpret films.

12. Film Criticism and Reviews:

- **Film Criticism:** Examination of critical approaches to evaluating and analyzing films.
- **Film Reviews:** Analysis of the role of film reviews in shaping audience perceptions and expectations.

Film studies is an interdisciplinary field that encourages critical thinking, cultural awareness, and an appreciation for the art and impact of cinema. It allows students and scholars to engage with a diverse range of films and explore how cinema reflects and shapes culture and society.

Film Production

Film production is the process of bringing a film from concept to completion. It involves numerous stages, each with its own set of tasks, professionals, and creative decisions. The filmmaking process can be broadly divided into pre-production, production, and post-production phases. Here's an overview of each stage:

1. **Pre-Production:**
   - Script Development:
     - The initial stage involves the creation and development of the screenplay or script. Writers, often in collaboration with directors, work on crafting the narrative, dialogue, and structure.
   - Project Planning:
     - Producers and production managers plan the entire project, considering budget constraints, scheduling, and resource allocation. They may create a production timeline and set financial parameters.
   - Casting:
     - Casting directors work to select actors who best fit the roles defined in the script. Auditions, callbacks, and negotiations with talent agents are part of this process.
   - Location Scouting:
     - The locations where filming will take place are scouted and chosen during this stage. This involves considering the visual and logistical aspects of each location.
   - Budgeting and Financing:
     - Producers create a budget that outlines the anticipated costs of the production. Funding may

come from various sources, including studios, investors, grants, and pre-sales.

- **Storyboarding and Shot Planning:**
    - Directors and cinematographers create storyboards or shot lists to plan the visual composition of each scene. This includes camera angles, movements, and key shots.
- **Hiring Crew:**
    - Key crew members, such as the director of photography, production designer, costume designer, and others, are hired during pre-production. The crew collaborates to bring the creative vision to life.
- **Legal and Permits:**
    - Legal aspects, including contracts, rights clearances, and obtaining necessary permits for filming, are addressed during pre-production.

2. Production:

- **Principal Photography:**
    - The actual shooting of the film takes place during the production phase. The director, actors, and various crew members work together to capture the scenes outlined in the script.
- **Set Operations:**
    - The production team manages various operations on set, including lighting, sound recording, makeup, costume changes, and set decoration.
- **Directing:**
    - The director oversees the creative aspects of the production, guiding actors, collaborating with the cinematographer, and making decisions that

contribute to the overall vision.
- Continuity and Script Supervision:
    - Continuity supervisors ensure consistency in visual and narrative elements from shot to shot. Script supervisors monitor dialogue and action to maintain continuity with the script.
- Data Management:
    - The camera crew and digital imaging technicians manage the recording and storage of audio-visual data during filming.
- Daily Wrap Reports:
    - At the end of each shooting day, the assistant director compiles a wrap report detailing the day's activities, any issues encountered, and plans for the next day.

3. Post-Production:

- Editing:
    - The editing process involves selecting and assembling the best takes, arranging them in chronological order, and refining the pacing and rhythm of the film. Editors collaborate with the director to achieve the desired narrative flow.
- Sound Design and Editing:
    - Sound designers and editors work on enhancing the auditory experience of the film. This includes adding dialogue, Foley effects, music, and ambient sounds.
- Visual Effects (VFX):
    - If the film requires visual effects, VFX artists create and integrate computer-generated elements into the live-action footage.
- Color Grading:

- - Colorists adjust and enhance the color and visual aesthetics of the film during the color grading process.
- **Music Composition and Scoring:**
  - Composers create original music or score for the film, enhancing emotional impact and supporting the narrative.
- **Screenings and Test Audiences:**
  - Filmmakers may organize test screenings to gather audience feedback, helping them make final adjustments to the film before its official release.
- **Final Cut and Mastering:**
  - The final cut of the film is locked, and the master version is created for distribution. This includes creating various versions for different formats and platforms.
- **Marketing and Promotion:**
  - Marketing teams develop strategies to promote the film, including trailers, posters, interviews, and social media campaigns.
- **Distribution:**
  - The film is distributed to theaters, online platforms, or other outlets, making it accessible to audiences.
- **Premiere and Release:**
  - The film has its premiere, and it is officially released for public viewing.

Additional Considerations:

- **Film Festivals:**
  - Some filmmakers choose to submit their films to festivals to gain exposure, recognition, and potential distribution deals.

- Awards and Recognition:
    - Successful films may receive nominations or awards at film festivals, industry events, or prestigious awards ceremonies.
- Archiving and Preservation:
    - Archiving and preserving the film elements are crucial for long-term access and historical documentation.

Film production is a collaborative and intricate process that involves the creativity and expertise of numerous professionals, each contributing to the final product. The journey from concept to screen requires careful planning, technical skills, artistic vision, and effective collaboration within the filmmaking team.

Film Analysis

Film analysis is the critical examination and interpretation of films as a form of art and cultural expression. It involves breaking down a film into its various components to understand how these elements contribute to the overall meaning and impact of the work. Film analysis considers aspects such as cinematography, editing, sound, narrative structure, themes, and cultural context. Here are key components and approaches to film analysis:

1. Cinematography:

- Camera Work:
    - Analyze the choices of camera angles, shots, and movements. Consider how these choices contribute to the storytelling and visual aesthetics.
- Composition:
    - Examine the framing and composition of shots. Pay attention to the use of space, balance, and visual elements within the frame.
- Lighting:
    - Evaluate the use of lighting techniques, including natural light, artificial lighting, and shadows, to create mood and atmosphere.

2. Editing:

- Pacing:
    - Consider the rhythm and pacing of the film. Analyze the editing choices in terms of the duration of shots, cuts, and transitions.
- Montage:
    - Explore how montage sequences are used to convey meaning, build tension, or establish thematic

connections between shots.

- Spatial and Temporal Relationships:
  - Examine how editing creates a sense of space and time within the narrative. Look for continuity editing and temporal manipulations.

3. Sound Design:

- Diegetic and Non-Diegetic Sound:
  - Analyze the use of sound within the film, distinguishing between sounds that are part of the story world (diegetic) and those added in post-production (non-diegetic).
- Music:
  - Consider the role of the film score or soundtrack in enhancing emotions, creating atmosphere, and supporting the narrative.

4. Narrative Structure:

- Three-Act Structure:
  - Identify the film's structure in terms of the traditional three-act model: setup, confrontation, and resolution.
- Flashbacks and Flashforwards:
  - Explore how non-linear narrative techniques, such as flashbacks or flashforwards, are employed to shape the storytelling.

5. Themes and Motifs:

- Identify Themes:
  - Analyze the underlying themes or messages conveyed by the film. Consider recurring motifs or symbols that contribute to the thematic elements.

- Character Motivations:
    - Examine the motivations and conflicts of the characters. How do their actions drive the narrative and contribute to the overall themes?

6. Genre Analysis:

- Genre Conventions:
    - Consider how the film adheres to or subverts genre conventions. Analyze how genre expectations influence audience perceptions.
- Hybrid Genres:
    - Explore films that blend multiple genres, analyzing how this blending impacts narrative and audience engagement.

7. Cultural and Historical Context:

- Social and Cultural Commentary:
    - Analyze how the film reflects or comments on social issues, cultural norms, or historical events.
- Genre and Period Influence:
    - Consider how the film's genre and the period in which it was made influence its themes, style, and narrative.

8. Auteur Theory:

- Director's Signature Style:
    - Apply auteur theory by examining the director's distinctive style, recurring themes, and directorial choices across their body of work.

9. Reception and Audience Response:

- Critical Reception:

- ○ Consider how the film was received by critics. Analyze reviews and scholarly interpretations.
- Audience Response:
  - ○ Explore how the film resonates with different audiences. Consider cultural, demographic, and contextual factors influencing audience reception.

10. Symbolism and Metaphor:

- Symbolic Elements:
  - ○ Identify symbolic elements, objects, or imagery in the film and analyze their meaning or significance.
- Metaphorical Interpretations:
  - ○ Consider how certain elements or scenes may have metaphorical or allegorical meanings beyond their literal representation.

Film analysis is subjective and open to interpretation. Various analytical frameworks and theories can be applied to deepen the understanding of a film's artistic, cultural, and narrative dimensions. Whether approached from a formalist, auteurist, feminist, Marxist, or other critical perspective, film analysis allows viewers and scholars to engage with films on a deeper level and appreciate the complexities of the cinematic medium.

Film History

Film history encompasses the development of cinema as an art form and an industry, covering the evolution of filmmaking techniques, genres, technology, and the cultural impact of films over time. The history of film is often divided into different periods, movements, and key developments. Here is an overview of significant milestones and eras in film history:

1. Pre-Cinema and Early Experiments (Late 19th Century):

- **Magic Lantern Shows:** Before the invention of film, magic lantern shows used projectors to display painted slides and create illusions.
- **Photographic and Optical Experiments:** Inventors like Eadweard Muybridge and Thomas Edison conducted experiments with sequential photographs and moving images.

2. Birth of Cinema (1890s-1900s):

- **Lumière Brothers:** In 1895, the Lumière Brothers held the first public screening of films using their Cinématographe in Paris. This event is considered the birth of cinema.
- **Early Narrative Films:** Filmmakers like Georges Méliès began experimenting with narrative storytelling and special effects.

3. Silent Film Era (1895-1929):

- **Pioneering Filmmakers:** D.W. Griffith, Charlie Chaplin, Buster Keaton, and others made significant contributions to silent film.
- **Film Genres:** Silent films explored various genres, including melodrama, comedy, horror, and epic films.

4. Introduction of Sound (1927-1930):

- **The Jazz Singer:** Al Jolson's "The Jazz Singer" (1927) was the first feature-length film with synchronized dialogue, marking the transition from silent to sound cinema.
- **Sound Technology:** The adoption of sound technology revolutionized filmmaking, leading to the decline of silent films.

5. Golden Age of Hollywood (1930s-1950s):

- **Studio System:** Hollywood studios, including MGM, Warner Bros., and Paramount, dominated the film industry.
- **Genres and Stars:** Classic genres like film noir, musicals, and westerns flourished. Icons like Clark Gable, Marilyn Monroe, and Humphrey Bogart became stars.
- **War Era:** World War II influenced film production, with patriotic and war-themed movies.

6. Post-War and Cold War Era (1940s-1960s):

- **Hollywood Ten and McCarthyism:** The Red Scare led to the Hollywood Ten blacklist, affecting filmmakers accused of having communist ties.
- **Television Impact:** The rise of television posed challenges to the film industry, leading to innovations like widescreen formats and 3D.

7. European New Wave (Late 1950s-1960s):

- **French New Wave:** Filmmakers like Jean-Luc Godard and François Truffaut embraced unconventional storytelling and influenced a new wave of cinema globally.
- **Italian Neorealism:** Directors like Vittorio De Sica and Roberto Rossellini focused on realistic portrayals of everyday life.

8. 1960s-1970s: Changing Landscapes:

- **New Hollywood:** A shift towards more innovative and socially relevant films emerged, including the works of directors like Francis Ford Coppola and Martin Scorsese.
- **Counterculture Movements:** Films of the 1960s and 1970s reflected the influence of counterculture movements and changing societal norms.

9. Blockbusters and Independent Cinema (1980s-Present):

- **Blockbuster Era:** The 1980s saw the rise of blockbuster filmmaking, with high-budget, special effects-laden films becoming prevalent.
- **Independent Cinema:** The 1990s and 2000s witnessed the growth of independent cinema, with directors like Quentin Tarantino and the Coen Brothers gaining prominence.

10. Digital Age and Globalization (Late 20th Century-Present):

- **Digital Technology:** The transition from analog to digital technology revolutionized film production, distribution, and exhibition.
- **Globalization:** Hollywood films became globally influential, while international cinema gained recognition through film festivals and awards.

11. 21st Century and Streaming Era:

- **Streaming Services:** The rise of streaming platforms like Netflix, Hulu, and Amazon Prime altered the distribution landscape.
- **Diversity and Inclusion:** Efforts to address diversity and inclusion in filmmaking gained momentum, with increased recognition of underrepresented voices.

12. Current Trends and Challenges:

- **Franchise Films:** The dominance of franchise films and cinematic universes has become a prominent trend.
- **Technological Advancements:** Virtual reality (VR), augmented reality (AR), and other technologies continue to influence filmmaking.
- **Pandemic Impact:** The COVID-19 pandemic brought significant challenges to film production and distribution.

Film history is a dynamic and evolving field that continues to be shaped by technological advancements, cultural shifts, and the creative contributions of filmmakers worldwide. Studying film history provides insights into the evolution of storytelling, visual language, and the broader cultural and social contexts in which films are created.

Cinematography

Cinematography is the art and technique of capturing moving images on film or digital media. It involves the use of camera and lighting to visually tell a story and create a certain mood or atmosphere. Cinematographers, also known as directors of photography (DPs), play a crucial role in shaping the visual aesthetics of a film. Here are key elements and techniques involved in cinematography:

1. Camera Movement:

- **Pan:** Horizontal movement of the camera on a fixed axis.
- **Tilt:** Vertical movement of the camera on a fixed axis.
- **Dolly/Tracking:** Movement of the entire camera towards or away from the subject.
- **Crane:** Vertical movement of the camera on an extending arm.

2. Composition:

- **Frame Composition:** Arranging visual elements within the frame for aesthetic and storytelling purposes.
- **Rule of Thirds:** Dividing the frame into a grid and placing important elements along the grid lines or intersections.

3. Framing:

- **Long Shot (LS):** Shows the subject from head to toe or in its entirety.
- **Medium Shot (MS):** Frames the subject from the waist up.
- **Close-Up (CU):** Isolates a specific part of the subject, such as the face or an object.
- **Extreme Close-Up (ECU):** Focuses on a very small detail or a portion of the subject.

4. Camera Angles:

- **High Angle:** Shooting from above, looking down on the subject. Can convey vulnerability or weakness.
- **Low Angle:** Shooting from below, looking up at the subject. Can create a sense of power or dominance.
- **Eye-Level:** Shooting at the same height as the subject. Provides a neutral and natural perspective.

5. Depth of Field:

- **Shallow Depth of Field:** Selective focus on a specific subject, with a blurred background. Emphasizes the subject and creates a cinematic look.
- **Deep Depth of Field:** Everything in the frame is in focus. Common in wide shots and certain styles of filmmaking.

6. Focus and Pulling Focus:

- **Focus Pulling:** Adjusting the focus during a shot to change the clarity of different subjects or areas within the frame.

7. Lens Choice:

- **Wide-Angle Lens:** Captures a broader view and exaggerates depth. Commonly used for establishing shots.
- **Normal Lens:** Represents a natural perspective similar to the human eye.
- **Telephoto Lens:** Brings distant subjects closer and compresses the perceived distance between objects.

8. Lighting:

- **Natural Light:** Using available light sources, such as the sun or moon.
- **Artificial Light:** Controlled use of lighting equipment to achieve specific effects.
- **Three-Point Lighting:** Key light, fill light, and backlight are used to illuminate the subject and provide depth.

9. Color Palette:

- **Color Grading:** The process of adjusting and enhancing the colors in post-production to achieve a specific visual tone or mood.

10. Aspect Ratio:

- **Aspect Ratio:** The ratio of the width to the height of the image. Different aspect ratios can impact the visual composition and storytelling.

11. Movement and Stabilization:

- **Handheld Camera:** Creates a sense of immediacy and intimacy.
- **Steadicam:** A stabilizing mount for the camera, allowing smooth movement without the shake of

handheld filming.

12. Blocking and Choreography:

- **Blocking:** Planning and coordinating the movement of actors and camera for a scene.
- **Choreography:** Coordination of camera movements with actions in the scene, such as fight scenes or dance sequences.

13. Cinematic Styles:

- **Realism:** Emphasizes a natural and unembellished representation of reality.
- **Expressionism:** Uses distorted visuals to evoke emotional or psychological responses.
- **Surrealism:** Departs from reality, often creating dreamlike or fantastical visuals.

14. Genre-specific Techniques:

- **Film Noir:** Dark, contrasty lighting; high-contrast compositions.
- **Horror:** Use of shadows, lighting contrasts, and unsettling compositions.
- **Science Fiction:** Futuristic settings, creative use of lighting, and special effects.

15. Collaboration with Other Departments:

- **Collaboration with Production Design:** Ensures visual consistency and alignment with the overall design.
- **Collaboration with Costume Design:** Ensures that costumes are properly showcased and contribute to the visual storytelling.

Cinematography is a dynamic and evolving field that involves creative choices, technical expertise, and collaboration with other filmmaking departments. The cinematographer works closely with the director to translate the script into a visual language that enhances the narrative and engages the audience.

Chapter 10

Intercultural Communication

Intercultural communication involves the exchange of information, ideas, and messages between individuals from different cultural backgrounds. It encompasses verbal and non-verbal communication, as well as how cultural differences impact the interpretation of messages. Effective intercultural communication is essential in a globalized world where people from diverse cultural backgrounds interact in various contexts such as business, education, healthcare, and social settings. Here are key aspects of intercultural communication:

1. Cultural Awareness:

- **Understanding Cultural Differences:** Being aware of and knowledgeable about the cultural norms, values, customs, and communication styles of different cultures.
- **Avoiding Stereotypes:** Recognizing that individuals within a culture can have diverse perspectives and avoiding generalized assumptions based on cultural stereotypes.

2. Verbal Communication:

- **Language Use:** Recognizing that language can be a source of both connection and misunderstanding. Consideration of language proficiency, accents, and idiomatic expressions is important.
- **Communication Styles:** Awareness of differences in directness, formality, and politeness in communication across cultures.

3. Non-Verbal Communication:

- **Body Language:** Understanding how gestures, facial expressions, and body language vary across cultures.
- **Proxemics:** Awareness of personal space preferences and the use of physical distance during interactions.

4. Cultural Context:

- **High-Context vs. Low-Context Cultures:** Understanding that some cultures rely heavily on contextual cues and implicit communication (high-context), while others emphasize explicit verbal communication (low-context).
- **Cultural References:** Recognizing that references to history, religion, and cultural symbols may carry

different meanings in different cultural contexts.

5. Cultural Sensitivity:

- **Empathy:** Being able to understand and share the feelings of individuals from other cultures.
- **Respect:** Showing respect for diverse perspectives, even when they differ from one's cultural norms.

6. Adaptability and Flexibility:

- **Adapting Communication Style:** Being flexible in adjusting communication styles to suit the cultural preferences and expectations of the audience.
- **Open-Mindedness:** Approaching intercultural interactions with an open mind and a willingness to learn.

7. Conflict Resolution:

- **Conflict Styles:** Understanding how different cultures approach and resolve conflicts. Some cultures may prefer confrontation, while others may value indirect methods.
- **Cultural Influences on Conflict:** Recognizing that cultural values and communication styles can influence the perception and resolution of conflicts.

8. Power Dynamics:

- **Hierarchy and Authority:** Understanding how power and authority are perceived in different cultures, and how this influences communication patterns.
- **Formality:** Recognizing the level of formality expected in various cultural settings, including the use of titles and proper etiquette.

9. Cross-Cultural Communication Competence:

- **Skills Development:** Actively working on developing intercultural communication competence through training, education, and exposure to diverse cultural experiences.
- **Feedback and Reflection:** Seeking feedback and reflecting on one's communication patterns to improve cross-cultural effectiveness.

10. Technology and Global Communication:

- **Virtual Communication:** Understanding the challenges and nuances of intercultural communication in

virtual environments, where individuals may be geographically distant.
- **Social Media:** Recognizing the impact of social media on intercultural communication and the potential for cultural misunderstandings.

11. Cultural Intelligence (CQ):

- **CQ Development:** Cultivating cultural intelligence, which involves the ability to adapt and function effectively in culturally diverse situations.

12. Education and Training:

- **Cultural Competency Training:** Providing education and training programs to enhance intercultural communication skills in various professional fields.

13. Diversity and Inclusion:

- **Promoting Inclusivity:** Fostering environments that celebrate diversity, promote inclusivity, and value contributions from individuals of different cultural backgrounds.

Effective intercultural communication is crucial for building positive relationships, fostering collaboration, and navigating the complexities of a multicultural world. It involves ongoing learning, curiosity, and a commitment to understanding and respecting the diversity of human experiences and perspectives.

Cross-Cultural Communication

Cross-cultural communication refers to the exchange of information and ideas between individuals from different cultural backgrounds. It involves understanding and navigating the complexities of diverse cultural norms, values, communication styles, and expectations. Successful cross-cultural communication is essential in various contexts, including business, education, healthcare, diplomacy, and interpersonal relationships. Here are key aspects and strategies related to cross-cultural communication:

1. Cultural Awareness and Sensitivity:

- **Understanding Cultural Differences:** Being aware of the variations in cultural norms, customs, and communication styles.
- **Cultural Sensitivity Training:** Engaging in training programs to enhance awareness and sensitivity to diverse cultural perspectives.

2. Communication Styles:

- **Direct vs. Indirect Communication:** Recognizing that some cultures prefer direct and explicit communication, while others value indirect and implicit communication.
- **High-Context vs. Low-Context Cultures:** Understanding the reliance on context and implicit cues in high-context cultures, as opposed to the explicit communication in low-context cultures.

3. Language Considerations:

- **Language Proficiency:** Being mindful of varying levels of proficiency in a shared language and adapting communication accordingly.
- **Use of Interpreters:** When necessary, use interpreters to ensure accurate and clear communication.

4. Non-Verbal Communication:

- **Body Language:** Understanding cultural variations in gestures, facial expressions, and body language.
- **Eye Contact and Personal Space:** Recognizing that cultural norms influence the appropriate use of eye contact and personal space.

5. Active Listening:

- **Listening Skills:** Developing active listening skills to understand not only the words spoken but also the cultural nuances and emotions conveyed.
- **Reflective Listening:** Paraphrasing and reflecting on what has been communicated to ensure mutual understanding.

6. Adaptability and Flexibility:

- **Cultural Adaptability:** Being adaptable and open to adjusting communication styles to align with the preferences and expectations of individuals from different cultures.
- **Flexibility in Business Practices:** Adjusting business practices and strategies to accommodate cultural differences.

7. Avoiding Stereotypes:

- **Cultural Stereotypes:** Avoiding the reliance on stereotypes and recognizing the diversity of individuals within any cultural group.
- **Individual Differences:** Acknowledging that individuals may have unique perspectives that deviate from cultural norms.

8. Empathy and Respect:

- **Cultural Empathy:** Putting oneself in the shoes of individuals from different cultures to understand their experiences and perspectives.
- **Respect for Cultural Differences:** Valuing and respecting cultural differences rather than imposing one's cultural norms.

9. Awareness of Power Dynamics:

- **Hierarchical Differences:** Understanding how power and authority are perceived and communicated in different cultures.
- **Navigating Power Imbalances:** Navigating conversations and interactions when there are differences in status or hierarchical structures.

10. Cross-Cultural Training Programs:

- **Professional Development:** Participating in cross-cultural training programs to develop skills and strategies for effective communication in diverse settings.

11. Global Virtual Communication:

- **Use of Technology:** Leveraging technology for virtual communication while being mindful of potential challenges, such as time zone differences and cultural nuances.
- **Building Relationships Online:** Nurturing relationships across cultures through virtual platforms.

12. Crisis Communication and Conflict Resolution:

- **Handling Conflicts:** Understanding how cultural differences may influence conflict resolution styles and adapting approaches accordingly.
- **Crisis Communication:** Effectively communicating during crises, considering cultural sensitivities and differences in communication norms.

13. Continuous Learning:

- **Curiosity and Open-Mindedness:** Cultivating a curious and open-minded attitude toward learning about new cultures and adapting to evolving cross-cultural dynamics.

14. Inclusive Communication Practices:

- **Inclusive Language:** Using inclusive language that acknowledges and respects diverse identities and perspectives.
- **Promoting Diversity and Inclusion:** Advocating for and contributing to environments that promote diversity and inclusion.

15. Feedback and Reflection:

- **Feedback Mechanisms:** Establishing mechanisms for providing and receiving feedback on cross-cultural communication to enhance learning and improvement.

Effective cross-cultural communication is an ongoing process that requires a combination of knowledge, skills, and a willingness to learn and adapt. It is a key factor in building positive relationships, fostering collaboration, and navigating the complexities of our increasingly interconnected world.

Global Media

Global media refers to the interconnected and transnational communication systems that disseminate information, entertainment, and cultural content across international borders. With the advent of advanced technologies and the rise of the internet, global media has become a powerful force in shaping public opinion, disseminating news, and influencing cultural exchange on a global scale. Here are key aspects of global media:

1. Media Convergence:

- **Integration of Technologies:** The convergence of various media platforms, such as print, television, radio, and the internet, into interconnected digital formats.
- **Multimedia Content:** The creation and distribution of content that spans multiple media formats, providing audiences with diverse and immersive experiences.

2. Global News Networks:

- **International News Agencies:** Organizations like Reuters, Associated Press (AP), and Agence France-Presse (AFP) disseminate news globally, contributing to a shared global news agenda.
- **Global News Networks:** Networks such as BBC World News, CNN International, and Al Jazeera English provide news coverage with a global perspective.

3. Social Media and Online Platforms:

- **Global Reach of Social Media:** Platforms like Facebook, Twitter, Instagram, and YouTube enable global communication, information sharing, and cultural exchange.
- **User-Generated Content:** The rise of user-generated content allows individuals worldwide to participate in creating and sharing media content.

4. Transnational Entertainment:

- **Global Film Industry:** Hollywood and other film industries produce movies that have international appeal and are distributed worldwide.
- **Television Shows and Streaming Services:** Platforms like Netflix, Amazon Prime, and Hulu provide

global audiences access to a wide range of television shows and films.

5. Global Advertising and Marketing:

- **Advertising Campaigns:** Global companies use international advertising campaigns to reach diverse audiences across different cultures.
- **Brand Presence:** Building a global brand presence through consistent messaging and marketing strategies.

6. Language and Localization:

- **Multilingual Content:** Creating content in multiple languages to cater to diverse linguistic audiences.
- **Localization Strategies:** Adapting content to local cultural norms, preferences, and sensitivities.

7. Global Journalism and Reporting:

- **International Correspondents:** News organizations deploy correspondents globally to provide in-depth reporting and analysis on international events.
- **Cross-Border Investigative Journalism:** Collaborative efforts among journalists and media outlets to investigate and report on global issues.

8. Cultural Exchange and Representation:

- **Diversity in Media Representation:** Efforts to promote diverse and inclusive representation in global media, reflecting a variety of cultures, ethnicities, and perspectives.
- **Cultural Diplomacy:** The use of media and cultural exchanges to foster understanding and goodwill between nations.

9. Global Media Regulations:

- **International Broadcasting Standards:** Organizations like the International Telecommunication Union (ITU) and the International Telecommunication Satellite Organization (ITSO) contribute to global broadcasting standards.
- **Regulatory Challenges:** Navigating diverse regulatory environments and addressing challenges related to content censorship and cultural sensitivities.

10. Media Literacy and Cross-Cultural Understanding:

- **Education and Awareness:** Promoting media literacy to help audiences critically evaluate and navigate global media content.
- **Understanding Cultural Nuances:** Encouraging an understanding of cultural nuances and context to interpret media messages accurately.

11. Digital Divide and Access:

- **Global Disparities in Access:** Addressing the digital divide to ensure equitable access to information and media technologies worldwide.
- **Digital Inclusion Initiatives:** Efforts to bridge gaps in digital access and promote inclusivity in global media participation.

12. Challenges of Misinformation and Fake News:

- **Dissemination of Misinformation:** Addressing the challenges posed by the rapid spread of misinformation and fake news on a global scale.
- **Media Literacy Programs:** Implementing educational programs to enhance critical thinking skills and media literacy to combat misinformation.

13. Crisis Communication and Global Events:

- **Media Coverage of Global Events:** The role of global media in providing coverage and disseminating information during major events such as natural disasters, pandemics, and geopolitical crises.
- **Humanitarian Communication:** The use of media to raise awareness and mobilize support for humanitarian causes and relief efforts.

14. Global Media Ethics:

- **Ethical Considerations:** Navigating ethical challenges in global media, including issues related to privacy, cultural sensitivity, and responsible journalism.
- **International Standards:** Adhering to and promoting international ethical standards in media practices.

Global media, with its wide reach and influence, plays a pivotal role in shaping public perceptions, fostering cross-cultural understanding, and contributing to the global exchange of ideas and information. The challenges and opportunities associated with global media require ongoing efforts to promote responsible and inclusive communication practices on an international scale.

Cultural Diversity in Media

Cultural diversity in media refers to the representation and inclusion of various cultural perspectives, identities, and backgrounds in the content and production of media. Embracing cultural diversity in media is crucial for reflecting the richness and complexity of the global population, promoting inclusivity, and challenging stereotypes. Here are key aspects and considerations related to cultural diversity in media:

1. Representation in Media Content:

- **Ethnic and Racial Diversity:** Ensuring that media content reflects the diversity of ethnic and racial backgrounds, avoiding stereotypes and tokenism.
- **Cultural Practices:** Depicting a variety of cultural practices, traditions, and lifestyles to present a more comprehensive view of different communities.

2. Inclusive Storytelling:

- **Diverse Narratives:** Encouraging the creation of narratives that authentically represent the experiences, challenges, and triumphs of individuals from various cultural backgrounds.
- **Intersectionality:** Recognizing and exploring the intersections of multiple identities, such as race, ethnicity, gender, and sexual orientation, within storytelling.

3. Representation Behind the Scenes:

- **Diverse Production Teams:** Encouraging diversity among writers, directors, producers, and other key roles in the media industry to ensure a variety of perspectives in storytelling.
- **Cultural Consultants:** Collaborating with cultural experts and consultants to ensure accurate and respectful portrayals of diverse cultures.

4. Language Diversity:

- **Multilingual Content:** Featuring content in different languages to reflect the linguistic diversity of global audiences.
- **Subtitles and Dubbing:** Providing accessibility through subtitles and dubbing to make content accessible

to audiences with diverse language backgrounds.

5. Promoting Underrepresented Voices:

- **Elevating Marginalized Communities:** Providing a platform for stories from historically marginalized and underrepresented communities.
- **Independent and Emerging Filmmakers:** Supporting independent and emerging filmmakers from diverse backgrounds to bring fresh perspectives to the industry.

6. News and Journalism:

- **Diverse News Sources:** Ensuring diverse representation in newsrooms and reporting to present a more comprehensive and nuanced understanding of global events.
- **Avoiding Stereotypes:** Responsible reporting that avoids perpetuating stereotypes and negative biases.

7. Cultural Competence in Marketing and Advertising:

- **Inclusive Marketing:** Creating advertising campaigns that resonate with diverse audiences and avoid cultural appropriation.
- **Authentic Representation:** Ensuring that advertisements reflect authentic cultural practices and values.

8. Children's and Educational Media:

- **Diversity in Children's Content:** Introducing diverse characters and storylines in children's programming to foster inclusivity and teach cultural understanding.
- **Educational Resources:** Developing educational media content that introduces children to a variety of cultures, histories, and perspectives.

9. Collaborations and Co-Productions:

- **International Collaborations:** Promoting collaborations between media professionals and organizations from different countries and cultural backgrounds.
- **Co-Productions:** Creating opportunities for joint productions that blend cultural influences and storytelling styles.

10. Cultural Sensitivity and Authenticity:

- **Research and Consultation:** Conducting thorough research and consulting with cultural experts to ensure accurate and respectful portrayals.

- **Feedback Loops:** Establishing mechanisms for feedback from diverse communities to address concerns and improve cultural representation.

11. Audience Engagement:

- **Community Engagement:** Involving diverse communities in the media-making process and seeking feedback from audiences.
- **Social Media Platforms:** Leveraging social media to connect with diverse audiences and amplify underrepresented voices.

12. Educational Initiatives:

- **Media Literacy Programs:** Implementing educational programs that teach audiences to critically analyze media, recognize stereotypes, and appreciate cultural diversity.
- **Training for Media Professionals:** Offering training programs to media professionals on cultural sensitivity, diversity, and inclusion.

13. Recognizing Cultural Holidays and Celebrations:

- **Incorporating Cultural Events:** Integrating cultural holidays, festivals, and celebrations into media content to showcase diverse cultural practices.
- **Avoiding Cultural Appropriation:** Being mindful of cultural sensitivities and avoiding the inappropriate use or appropriation of cultural symbols and practices.

Cultural diversity in media is not only a matter of representation but also a powerful tool for fostering understanding, empathy, and appreciation for different cultures. Embracing diversity contributes to the creation of a more inclusive and reflective media landscape that resonates with diverse audiences worldwide.

Chapter 11

Media and Society

The relationship between media and society is complex and dynamic, with media playing a significant role in shaping, reflecting, and influencing various aspects of society. The impact of media on society is multidimensional, encompassing cultural, social, political, economic, and individual dimensions. Here are key considerations regarding the interplay between media and society:

1. Information Dissemination:

- **News and Journalism:** Media serves as a primary source of news and information, shaping public perception of current events and issues.
- **Role in Democracy:** Media plays a crucial role in a democratic society by providing citizens with information necessary for informed decision-making.

2. Cultural Influence:

- **Cultural Representation:** Media reflects and contributes to the construction of cultural norms, values, and identities.
- **Popular Culture:** Media, including television, films, music, and literature, significantly influences popular culture and societal trends.

3. Socialization and Identity Formation:

- **Media and Socialization:** Media plays a role in socializing individuals, especially through the representation of societal norms and values.
- **Identity Construction:** Media contributes to the construction of personal and collective identities, influencing how individuals perceive themselves and others.

4. Political Influence:

- **Agenda Setting:** Media influences public agendas by highlighting specific issues and framing discussions around particular topics.
- **Political Campaigns:** Media is a crucial platform for political communication, shaping public opinion during election campaigns.

5. Economic Impact:

- **Advertising and Consumerism:** Media, through advertising, drives consumer culture and influences purchasing behavior.
- **Media Industries:** The media sector itself is a significant economic force, contributing to employment, innovation, and economic growth.

6. Technological Advancements:

- **Digital Revolution:** Technological advancements, particularly the rise of the internet and digital media, have transformed the media landscape, affecting how information is produced, consumed, and shared.
- **Social Media:** Platforms like Facebook, Twitter, and Instagram have redefined communication patterns and allowed for widespread participation in information dissemination.

7. Media Literacy:

- **Critical Thinking Skills:** Media literacy is essential for developing critical thinking skills, enabling individuals to evaluate and interpret media content.
- **Navigating Information Overload:** Media literacy helps individuals navigate the abundance of information available and discern credible sources.

8. Cultural and Social Movements:

- **Social Activism:** Media platforms play a crucial role in facilitating and amplifying social and cultural movements by providing a space for advocacy and mobilization.
- **Cultural Expression:** Media provides a platform for diverse cultural expressions, fostering inclusivity and representation.

9. Globalization of Media:

- **Cross-Border Communication:** Global media allows for the exchange of information and cultural content across national boundaries.
- **Cultural Diversity:** Global media contributes to the dissemination of diverse cultural products and perspectives.

10. Media Regulation and Ethics:

- **Regulatory Frameworks:** Governments and regulatory bodies may establish frameworks to govern

media practices, addressing issues like content standards, ownership, and competition.
- **Ethical Standards:** Adherence to ethical standards in media, including accuracy, fairness, and respect for privacy, is essential for maintaining public trust.

11. Public Opinion and Perception:

- **Framing and Agenda Setting:** Media framing shapes public perception by emphasizing certain aspects of an issue and influencing the agenda.
- **Media Bias:** Awareness of media bias is crucial, as it can impact public opinion through the selection and presentation of information.

12. Media and Power Structures:

- **Media Ownership:** Concentration of media ownership can influence the diversity of voices and perspectives in the media landscape.
- **Role in Social Hierarchies:** Media can either challenge or reinforce existing social hierarchies, depending on the content and representation.

13. Entertainment and Escapism:

- **Role of Entertainment Media:** Entertainment media, including films, television shows, and video games, provides escapism and contributes to cultural and social leisure.
- **Cultural Impact of Entertainment:** Entertainment media has a profound impact on cultural norms, values, and trends.

14. Crisis Communication:

- **Role in Crisis Situations:** Media plays a critical role in disseminating information during crises, such as natural disasters, public health emergencies, and conflicts.
- **Challenges of Misinformation:** Managing and combating misinformation during crises is a significant challenge for media and society.

15. Individual and Collective Influence:

- **Personal Consumption:** Individual media consumption habits contribute to shaping personal beliefs, preferences, and behaviors.
- **Social Influence:** Media influences societal attitudes and behaviors, contributing to collective norms and

values.

Understanding the intricate relationship between media and society is essential for fostering a media environment that serves the public interest, promotes cultural diversity, and facilitates informed civic engagement. It requires ongoing dialogue, media literacy efforts, and a commitment to ethical and responsible media practices.

Media Influence on Society

The influence of media on society is profound and multifaceted, encompassing various aspects of individuals' lives, culture, politics, and public opinion. Media, in its various forms, plays a significant role in shaping perceptions, disseminating information, and influencing behaviors. Here are key ways in which media exerts influence on society:

1. Shaping Public Opinion:

- **Agenda Setting:** Media influences what topics are considered important and deserving of attention, shaping public agendas and priorities.
- **Framing:** The way media frames news stories can impact how audiences perceive and interpret issues, influencing public opinion.

2. Cultural Influence:

- **Cultural Representation:** Media reflects and contributes to the construction of cultural norms, values, and identities.
- **Cultural Trends:** Media, particularly entertainment media, influences cultural trends, fashion, and lifestyle choices.

3. Socialization and Identity Formation:

- **Role in Socialization:** Media contributes to socialization by presenting societal norms, values, and behaviors.
- **Identity Construction:** Media influences how individuals perceive themselves and others, contributing to the construction of personal and collective identities.

4. Political Impact:

- **Political Communication:** Media serves as a platform for political communication, influencing public opinion and electoral outcomes.
- **Political Agenda:** Media can shape political agendas by highlighting specific issues and influencing the public discourse.

5. Economic Influence:

- **Advertising and Consumerism:** Media, through advertising, influence consumer behavior, driving economic activity and shaping purchasing decisions.
- **Economic Reporting:** Media reporting on economic conditions can impact public confidence, investment, and financial markets.

6. Technological Advancements:

- **Digital Revolution:** The rise of the internet and digital media has transformed the way information is produced, distributed, and consumed.
- **Social Media Influence:** Platforms like Facebook, Twitter, and Instagram have redefined communication patterns and facilitated information sharing.

7. Public Awareness and Education:

- **Informative Role:** Media serves as a primary source of information, raising awareness on various issues, including health, science, and education.
- **Educational Content:** Educational programs and documentaries contribute to public knowledge and understanding.

8. Media Literacy and Opinion Formation:

- **Critical Thinking Skills:** Media literacy is crucial for developing critical thinking skills, enabling individuals to evaluate and interpret media content.
- **Opinion Formation:** Media shapes individual and collective opinions through its presentation and interpretation of information.

9. Globalization of Information:

- **Cross-Border Communication:** Media facilitates the exchange of information and cultural content across national boundaries, contributing to globalization.
- **Global Perspectives:** Access to international news sources provides audiences with diverse global perspectives.

10. Social Movements and Activism:

- **Facilitating Movements:** Media platforms play a crucial role in facilitating and amplifying social and

cultural movements by providing a space for advocacy and mobilization.
- **Awareness Campaigns:** Media is used for awareness campaigns related to social justice, human rights, and environmental issues.

11. Aggression and Violence:

- **Media Influence on Behavior:** Exposure to violent or aggressive content in media has been linked to changes in behavior, particularly in children and adolescents.
- **Media Desensitization:** Prolonged exposure to violent media may desensitize individuals to real-world violence.

12. Political Socialization:

- **Political Beliefs:** Media plays a role in shaping political beliefs, attitudes, and affiliations from an early age, contributing to political socialization.
- **Media Bias:** Awareness of media bias is essential, as it can impact political perceptions and preferences.

13. Celebrity Influence:

- **Celebrity Culture:** Media contributes to the creation and perpetuation of celebrity culture, influencing public attitudes, trends, and aspirations.
- **Endorsements and Trends:** Celebrity endorsements in media can impact consumer choices and popular trends.

14. Crisis Communication:

- **Role in Crisis Situations:** Media plays a critical role in disseminating information during crises, such as natural disasters, public health emergencies, and conflicts.
- **Challenges of Misinformation:** Managing and combating misinformation during crises is a significant challenge for media and society.

15. Media Regulation and Ethics:

- **Regulatory Frameworks:** Governments and regulatory bodies may establish frameworks to govern media practices, addressing issues like content standards, ownership, and competition.
- **Ethical Standards:** Adherence to ethical standards in media, including accuracy, fairness, and respect for privacy, is essential for maintaining public trust.

While the media's influence on society can be positive, empowering, and informative, it also comes with challenges and risks, such as misinformation, sensationalism, and the potential to reinforce stereotypes. Media literacy, ethical journalism, and responsible media practices are crucial for mitigating these challenges and ensuring a positive impact on society.

Media and Democracy

The relationship between media and democracy is integral to the functioning of democratic societies. A free and independent media is often considered a cornerstone of democracy, playing several key roles in ensuring the health and vitality of democratic systems. Here is how media interacts with and contributes to democracy:

1. Informing and Educating Citizens:

- **News and Information:** Media serves as a primary source of news and information, providing citizens with the knowledge needed for informed decision-making.
- **Educational Content:** Media contributes to public education by presenting diverse perspectives, analyses, and background information on various issues.

2. Facilitating Public Debate:

- **Open Forum for Discussion:** Media platforms provide spaces for public discourse and debate on political, social, and economic matters.
- **Editorials and Opinions:** Editorial content and opinion pieces contribute to the diversity of views and ideas presented to the public.

3. Agenda-Setting and Framing:

- **Agenda-Setting Role:** Media influences public agendas by determining which issues are emphasized and discussed.
- **Framing Discussions:** The way media frames news stories can shape public perceptions and understanding of political events and issues.

4. Political Watchdog Function:

- **Investigative Journalism:** Media acts as a check on power by conducting investigations into government actions, exposing corruption, and holding officials accountable.
- **Whistleblower Support:** Media provides a platform for whistleblowers to bring forth information about government misconduct.

5. Electoral Coverage:

- **Political Campaigns:** Media plays a crucial role in covering political campaigns, debates, and elections, providing voters with information about candidates and their platforms.
- **Access to Candidates:** Interviews, debates, and candidate forums facilitated by the media allow voters to assess the qualifications and positions of those seeking office.

6. Public Accountability:

- **Government Transparency:** Media promotes transparency by reporting on government activities, policies, and decision-making processes.
- **Public Scrutiny:** Public officials are subject to scrutiny and accountability through media coverage, fostering a responsive and responsible government.

7. Media Pluralism:

- **Diverse Media Outlets:** A plurality of media outlets ensures that a wide range of voices and perspectives are represented, preventing the concentration of media power.
- **Independent Journalism:** Independent media outlets contribute to the diversity of news coverage and investigative reporting.

8. Civic Engagement:

- **Encouraging Participation:** Media encourages civic engagement by informing citizens about civic duties, rights, and opportunities for involvement.
- **Coverage of Civil Society:** Media covers the activities of civil society organizations, grassroots movements, and community initiatives.

9. Free Speech and Expression:

- **Protection of Free Speech:** A democratic society values and protects the freedom of expression, allowing media to operate independently and without undue censorship.
- **Dissent and Opposition Voices:** Media provides a platform for dissenting and opposition voices, fostering a robust marketplace of ideas.

10. Media Literacy:

- **Informed Citizenship:** Media literacy education helps citizens critically evaluate media content, discern credible sources, and navigate information in a democratic society.

- **Resisting Disinformation:** Media literacy empowers individuals to recognize and resist the spread of misinformation and fake news.

11. Social Media and Democracy:

- **Facilitating Public Discourse:** Social media platforms enable the rapid dissemination of information and facilitate public discussions on a wide range of topics.
- **Challenges of Misinformation:** Social media also poses challenges, such as the spread of misinformation, echo chambers, and the manipulation of public opinion.

12. Challenges and Risks:

- **Media Ownership and Bias:** Concentration of media ownership and bias can limit the diversity of voices and perspectives.
- **Political Manipulation:** Media can be susceptible to political manipulation, and misinformation campaigns can influence public opinion.

13. International Dimension:

- **Global Information Exchange:** Media facilitates the exchange of information and perspectives across borders, contributing to a global understanding of democratic principles.
- **Global Advocacy:** Media coverage and international reporting can bring attention to human rights abuses and promote democratic values globally.

14. Media Regulation and Press Freedom:

- **Balancing Regulation:** Democracies aim to balance the need for media regulation to ensure responsible journalism with the preservation of press freedom.
- **Protection of Journalists:** Ensuring the safety and protection of journalists is crucial for upholding press freedom and the watchdog function.

15. Media and Public Trust:

- **Building Trust:** A democratic society relies on a media ecosystem that prioritizes accuracy, fairness, and transparency to build and maintain public trust.
- **Erosion of Trust:** Misinformation, sensationalism, and perceived bias can erode public trust in media institutions.

While the relationship between media and democracy is generally positive, ongoing challenges and debates exist, such as the need for media literacy, the impact of new technologies, and the role of social media in shaping public discourse. Striking a balance between media freedom, responsibility, and accountability is essential for a healthy and vibrant democratic society.

Media and Social Change

Media plays a crucial role in driving and reflecting social change. It has the power to shape public opinion, influence cultural norms, and contribute to movements that seek to bring about positive transformations in society. Here are key ways in which media intersects with social change:

1. Raising Awareness:

- **Social Issues:** Media brings attention to various social issues, including poverty, inequality, discrimination, and environmental concerns.
- **Human Rights Violations:** Coverage of human rights abuses and injustices helps raise awareness and mobilize support for change.

2. Advocacy and Activism:

- **Platform for Activism:** Media provides a platform for activists and advocacy groups to share their messages, organize campaigns, and mobilize public support.
- **Amplifying Voices:** Social media, in particular, amplifies grassroots movements and allows marginalized voices to be heard.

3. Cultural Shifts:

- **Representation in Media:** Positive representation of diverse groups in media contributes to cultural shifts and challenges stereotypes.
- **Inclusive Storytelling:** Media content that reflects diverse experiences and perspectives fosters understanding and empathy.

4. Changing Attitudes and Norms:

- **Portrayal of Social Norms:** Media influences societal attitudes by either reinforcing or challenging prevailing social norms.
- **LGBTQ+ Rights:** Media representation has played a role in changing public perceptions and attitudes toward LGBTQ+ rights.

5. Educational Content:

- **Informative Programming:** Educational media content contributes to awareness and understanding of important social issues.
- **Documentaries and Features:** Media productions, such as documentaries, can provide in-depth explorations of social challenges and solutions.

6. Social Movements:

- **Media Coverage:** Media plays a key role in covering and disseminating information about social movements, from civil rights movements to environmental activism.
- **Digital Activism:** Online platforms enable the rapid spread of information, making it easier for movements to gain traction and influence public opinion.

7. Crisis Communication:

- **Humanitarian Crises:** Media coverage of humanitarian crises mobilizes public support, fosters empathy, and prompts action.
- **Disaster Response:** Media plays a vital role in disseminating information during natural disasters and emergencies.

8. Public Health Campaigns:

- **Health Awareness:** Media campaigns contribute to public health initiatives by raising awareness about issues like disease prevention, mental health, and healthy lifestyles.
- **Changing Behaviors:** Social marketing through media channels encourages positive health behaviors and discourages harmful practices.

9. Environmental Awareness:

- **Climate Change:** Media, including documentaries and news coverage, contributes to raising awareness about environmental issues, climate change, and sustainable practices.
- **Environmental Activism:** Media platforms provide a means for environmental activists to share information and mobilize support.

10. Technology and Social Innovation:

- **Digital Platforms:** Technology and social media platforms facilitate social innovation, connecting individuals and organizations working toward positive change.

- **Crowdsourcing and Collaboration:** Media enables collaborative efforts, crowdsourcing, and the sharing of ideas for social impact.

11. Challenges to the Status Quo:

- **Investigative Journalism:** Media outlets play a crucial role in exposing corruption, abuses of power, and systemic injustices through investigative reporting.
- **Challenging Authority:** Media serves as a check on authority and can challenge the status quo, fostering accountability.

12. Promotion of Diversity and Inclusion:

- **Representation Matters:** Media representation influences societal perceptions of diversity and inclusion, challenging biases and stereotypes.
- **Promoting Equality:** Media can advocate for equal rights, social justice, and policies that promote inclusivity.

13. Community Empowerment:

- **Local Media:** Community-based media platforms empower local communities by providing a voice for local issues and concerns.
- **Storytelling for Change:** Personal stories shared through media platforms can inspire empathy and motivate collective action.

14. Media Literacy for Social Change:

- **Empowering Audiences:** Media literacy programs empower individuals to critically analyze media messages and be active contributors to positive social change.
- **Resisting Misinformation:** Media literacy skills help individuals discern credible information from misinformation and disinformation.

15. Social and Economic Justice:

- **Economic Inequality:** Media can shed light on economic disparities and advocate for policies that address social and economic justice.
- **Labor Movements:** Media plays a role in covering labor movements and advocating for workers' rights and fair labor practices.

While media has the potential to drive positive social change, it's essential to acknowledge that media can also perpetuate negative influences or reinforce existing power structures. Responsible journalism, ethical practices, and media literacy are crucial elements for leveraging media's potential for a positive impact on society.

Media and Identity

Media plays a significant role in shaping individual and collective identities by influencing how people perceive themselves and others. It contributes to the construction, reinforcement, and negotiation of various aspects of identity, including cultural, gender, racial, ethnic, and national identities. Here are key ways in which media intersects with identity:

1. Cultural Identity:

- **Representation:** Media influences the representation of different cultures, contributing to the formation of cultural identities.
- **Cultural Expression:** Through various media forms, individuals express and engage with their cultural identities, fostering a sense of belonging.

2. Gender Identity:

- **Gender Roles and Stereotypes:** Media shapes perceptions of gender roles and reinforces or challenges stereotypes, influencing how individuals perceive and express their gender identities.
- **Representation in Media:** The representation of diverse gender identities in media can contribute to greater visibility and understanding.

3. Racial and Ethnic Identity:

- **Representation and Stereotypes:** Media representation of racial and ethnic groups can influence how people perceive themselves and others, either reinforcing stereotypes or challenging them.
- **Cultural Heritage:** Media can be a platform for celebrating and preserving cultural heritage, contributing to the affirmation of racial and ethnic identities.

4. National Identity:

- **Media Narratives:** Media narratives contribute to the construction of national identity by shaping how history, values, and cultural symbols are portrayed.
- **News and Patriotism:** News media can play a role in shaping patriotic sentiments and perceptions of national identity during times of crisis or conflict.

5. Sexual and LGBTQ+ Identity:

- **Representation and Visibility:** Media representation of diverse sexual orientations and gender identities contributes to increased visibility and understanding.
- **Portrayal of Relationships:** Media can shape perceptions of different types of relationships, fostering acceptance and challenging stereotypes.

6. Age and Generational Identity:

- **Generational Narratives:** Media reflects and shapes generational narratives, influencing how different age groups perceive themselves and are perceived by others.
- **Youth Culture:** Media plays a significant role in the development and dissemination of youth culture, impacting generational identities.

7. Social Class Identity:

- **Economic Narratives:** Media portrays and reinforces narratives related to social class, influencing perceptions of economic status and social mobility.
- **Consumer Culture:** Advertising and media often reflect and shape consumer culture, influencing how individuals express social class identity.

8. Intersectionality:

- **Intersecting Identities:** Media can address or overlook intersecting identities, such as those related to race, gender, sexuality, and disability, affecting the complex ways individuals experience identity.
- **Representation Challenges:** Ensuring accurate and diverse representations across intersecting identities is an ongoing challenge for media.

9. Digital Identity:

- **Online Presence:** Social media and digital platforms play a role in the construction of digital identities, with individuals curating and expressing aspects of themselves online.
- **Online Communities:** Online spaces contribute to the formation of virtual communities that share common interests or identities.

10. Body Image and Identity:

- **Media Influence on Beauty Standards:** Media, including advertising and entertainment, influences

perceptions of beauty standards, impacting body image and self-esteem.
- **Body Positivity Movements:** Media can also be a platform for promoting body positivity and challenging narrow beauty norms.

11. Language and Linguistic Identity:

- **Media Language Use:** Language choices in media contribute to the shaping of linguistic identity, including the use of specific dialects, accents, or languages.
- **Multilingual Media:** The portrayal of multilingualism in media reflects linguistic diversity and influences language identity.

12. Narratives of Migration and Diaspora:

- **Migration Stories:** Media narratives play a role in shaping perceptions of migration, diaspora experiences, and the formation of transnational identities.
- **Cultural Hybridity:** Media can reflect cultural hybridity and the blending of identities in diasporic communities.

13. Identity Exploration in Media:

- **Media as a Mirror and Window:** Media serves as both a mirror reflecting one's identity and a window offering glimpses into diverse identities, fostering understanding and empathy.
- **Character Development:** Fictional characters in media contribute to identity exploration by providing relatable or aspirational figures.

14. Identity and Social Media Influencers:

- **Influence on Lifestyle and Values:** Social media influencers can impact the formation of identity by shaping lifestyle choices, values, and aspirational goals.
- **Connection and Community:** Influencers can create online communities that foster a sense of belonging and shared identity among their followers.

15. Challenges and Critiques:

- **Stereotyping and Misrepresentation:** Media can perpetuate stereotypes and misrepresentations, leading to challenges in how certain groups are perceived.
- **Cultural Appropriation:** The appropriation of cultural elements in media can raise concerns about the

misrepresentation and commodification of cultural identity.

Understanding the complex relationship between media and identity involves critical examination, awareness of biases, and ongoing efforts to promote diverse and authentic representations. Media has the potential to both reflect and shape identities, and its responsible use can contribute to a more inclusive and understanding society.

Chapter 12

Media Research

Media research encompasses a wide range of studies and investigations focused on understanding the various aspects of media, its effects, and its role in society. Scholars and researchers employ diverse methodologies to explore topics within the field of media. Here are key areas and methods associated with media research:

Areas of Media Research:

1. **Media Effects:**
    - Examining how media influences attitudes, beliefs, behaviors, and perceptions.
2. **Media Content Analysis:**
    - Analyzing the content of media messages, identifying patterns, themes, and representations.
3. **Media Literacy:**
    - Investigating the level of media literacy in different populations and the impact of media literacy programs.
4. **Media and Society:**
    - Studying the relationship between media and societal structures, norms, and changes.
5. **Media and Politics:**
    - Researching the role of media in political communication, elections, and public opinion formation.
6. **Media and Culture:**
    - Exploring the influence of media on cultural norms, values, and cultural production.
7. **Media and Technology:**
    - Investigating the impact of technological advancements on media consumption patterns and

media industries.
8. **Media and Identity:**
    - Studying how media contributes to the construction and negotiation of individual and collective identities.
9. **Media Economics:**
    - Analyzing the economic aspects of media industries, including advertising, revenue models, and market dynamics.
10. **Media Regulation:**
    - Investigating regulatory frameworks and policies governing media practices.
11. **Media History:**
    - Research historical developments and changes in media forms, technologies, and industries.
12. **Social Media Research:**
    - Exploring user behavior, trends, and the impact of social media on communication and society.
13. **Media and Globalization:**
    - Studying the role of media in the interconnected global landscape.
14. **Media Convergence:**
    - Investigating the merging of different media forms and platforms.
15. **Media and Health Communication:**
    - Researching how media influences health-related behaviors, perceptions, and communication.

Methods in Media Research:

1. **Surveys and Questionnaires:**
    - Collecting quantitative data on media consumption patterns, preferences, and opinions.

2. **Content Analysis:**
    - Systematically analyzing media content to identify patterns, themes, and trends.
3. **Interviews:**
    - Conducting in-depth interviews with individuals to explore their experiences, attitudes, and perspectives related to media.
4. **Focus Groups:**
    - Bringing together a group of individuals to discuss and share their opinions on media-related topics.
5. **Experimental Research:**
    - Conducting controlled experiments to measure the effects of specific media stimuli on participants.
6. **Ethnography:**
    - Immersing researchers in a particular media or cultural context to observe and understand behaviors and practices.
7. **Case Studies:**
    - In-depth examination of a specific media case, industry, or phenomenon.
8. **Longitudinal Studies:**
    - Tracking changes over time by collecting data from the same individuals or groups at multiple points.
9. **Big Data Analysis:**
    - Analyzing large datasets, often obtained from digital platforms, to identify patterns and trends.
10. **Qualitative Analysis:**
    - Using qualitative research methods, such as thematic analysis or discourse analysis, to explore media-related phenomena.
11. **Historical Research:**
    - Examining historical documents and archives to

understand the evolution of media over time.
12. **Participant Observation:**
    - Researchers actively participating in or observing media-related activities to gain insights.
13. **Cultural Studies:**
    - Applying interdisciplinary approaches to study media within broader cultural contexts.
14. **Usability Testing:**
    - Evaluating the user experience and effectiveness of media interfaces and technologies.
15. **Network Analysis:**
    - Examining the structure and dynamics of media networks, especially in the context of social media.

Media research is a dynamic field that evolves with technological advancements, changes in media consumption patterns, and shifts in societal norms. Researchers use a combination of quantitative and qualitative methods to explore the multifaceted nature of media and its impact on individuals and societies.

Research Methods in Communication

Research methods in communication encompass a variety of approaches used to investigate, analyze, and understand communication processes, phenomena, and effects. Researchers in communication employ diverse methodologies, ranging from quantitative to qualitative, to explore different aspects of human communication. Here are key research methods commonly used in communication studies:

Quantitative Research Methods:

1. **Surveys:**
    - **Description:** Surveys involve collecting data through structured questionnaires or interviews from a sample of respondents.
    - **Application:** Used to measure attitudes, behaviors, and opinions on communication-related topics.
2. **Experiments:**
    - **Description:** Controlled investigations manipulating variables to examine cause-and-effect relationships.
    - **Application:** Used to study the impact of specific communication stimuli on attitudes or behaviors.
3. **Content Analysis:**
    - **Description:** Systematic analysis of the content of communication artifacts (e.g., texts, images, videos).
    - **Application:** Used to identify patterns, themes, and trends in media content or communication messages.
4. **Observational Research:**
    - **Description:** Directly observing and recording

communication behaviors in natural settings.
    - **Application:** Used to understand interpersonal communication, nonverbal behavior, or group dynamics.
5. **Ex Post Facto Research:**
    - **Description:** Examining relationships between variables that cannot be manipulated.
    - **Application:** Used when experimental manipulation is not feasible, such as studying the effects of pre-existing characteristics.
6. **Meta-Analysis:**
    - **Description:** Statistical analysis that combines results from multiple studies on the same topic.
    - **Application:** Used to synthesize findings, identify patterns, and assess the overall effect of communication interventions.

Qualitative Research Methods:

1. **Interviews:**
    - **Description:** In-depth, semi-structured, or unstructured conversations with participants.
    - **Application:** Used to explore complex topics, attitudes, and experiences in depth.
2. **Focus Groups:**
    - **Description:** Group discussions with participants guided by a moderator to gather insights.
    - **Application:** Useful for exploring diverse perspectives on communication-related topics.
3. **Ethnography:**
    - **Description:** Immersion in a cultural or social

setting to understand communication practices.
- **Application:** Used to study communication within specific contexts or communities.

4. **Case Studies:**
    - **Description:** In-depth analysis of a particular case, event, or phenomenon.
    - **Application:** Provides detailed insights into specific communication occurrences.

5. **Grounded Theory:**
    - **Description:** Inductive approach to generating theories from qualitative data.
    - **Application:** Used to develop theoretical frameworks based on observed communication patterns.

6. **Narrative Analysis:**
    - **Description:** Examination of the stories people tell to understand communication patterns.
    - **Application:** Used to explore how individuals construct and convey meaning through narratives.

7. **Discourse Analysis:**
    - **Description:** Examination of language use in communication, considering social and cultural contexts.
    - **Application:** Used to understand power dynamics, social identities, and discursive practices.

8. **Visual Communication Analysis:**
    - **Description:** Examination of visual elements, such as images or symbols, in communication.
    - **Application:** Used to explore the impact of visuals on meaning and perception.

Mixed Methods:

1. **Sequential Explanatory Design:**
   - **Description:** A two-phase design where qualitative data collection and analysis follow quantitative data collection.
   - **Application:** Used to provide a comprehensive understanding of a communication phenomenon.
2. **Convergent Design:**
   - **Description:** Simultaneous collection of both quantitative and qualitative data, with integration during analysis.
   - **Application:** Offers a holistic perspective on a communication issue.
3. **Embedded Design:**
   - **Description:** One form of data collection is embedded within another, with separate analysis.
   - **Application:** Combines the strengths of both methods for a more comprehensive understanding.
4. **Transformative Design:**
   - **Description:** Integration of quantitative and qualitative data with an emphasis on transformative insights.
   - **Application:** Used to generate practical solutions or interventions based on research findings.

Communication researchers select methods based on their research questions, the nature of the phenomenon under study, and the desired depth of understanding. Often, researchers may combine methods to gain a more comprehensive view of communication processes and outcomes.

Media Audience Analysis

Media audience analysis involves examining the characteristics, behaviors, preferences, and attitudes of the audience that consumes media content. Understanding the audience is crucial for media producers, advertisers, and content creators to tailor their messages effectively. Here are the key components of media audience analysis:

Demographics:

1. **Age:**
   - **Understanding Age Groups:** Analyzing the age distribution of the audience helps tailor content to specific age demographics.

2. **Gender:**
   - **Gender-Based Preferences:** Examining how different genders engage with and respond to media content.

3. **Geography:**
   - **Regional Variances:** Understanding regional preferences and tailoring content to specific geographic areas.

4. **Income:**
   - **Economic Segmentation:** Analyzing the income levels of the audience to tailor content and advertisements.

5. **Education:**
   - **Educational Background:** Understanding the educational levels of the audience to gauge content comprehension.

6. **Occupation:**
   - **Professional Segmentation:** Examining the occupational background of the audience for targeted content.

7. **Family Status:**
   - **Family Composition:** Understanding the family structure to create content relevant to different family types.

Psychographics:

1. **Lifestyle:**
   - **Lifestyle Choices:** Analyzing the interests, hobbies, and lifestyle choices of the audience.
2. **Values and Beliefs:**
   - **Cultural and Social Values:** Understanding the cultural and social values that resonate with the audience.
3. **Personality Traits:**
   - **Personality-Based Preferences:** Examining how different personality traits correlate with media consumption.
4. **Attitudes:**
   - **Attitude Analysis:** Assessing the audience's attitudes toward various topics and issues.
5. **Opinions:**
   - **Opinion Formation:** Understanding how media consumption influences the formation of opinions.

Behavioral Patterns:

1. **Media Consumption Habits:**
   - **Preferred Platforms:** Identifying the platforms and channels the audience uses for consuming media.
2. **Content Preferences:**
   - **Genre Preferences:** Analyzing preferences for specific genres or types of content.
3. **Engagement Levels:**
   - **Interaction with Content:** Understanding how actively the audience engages with media content (e.g., likes, shares, comments).
4. **Media Usage Time:**
   - **Time-of-Day Analysis:** Examining when the audience is most active in consuming media.
5. **Multitasking:**
   - **Simultaneous Media Use:** Understanding whether the audience engages with multiple media simultaneously.

Technographic Factors:

1. **Device Usage:**

- **Preferred Devices:** Analyzing whether the audience prefers consuming content on smartphones, tablets, computers, or traditional media.

2. **Digital Literacy:**
   - **Technological Proficiency:** Understanding the audience's comfort level with digital technologies.

3. **Social Media Presence:**
   - **Platform Preferences:** Identifying which social media platforms the audience actively uses.

Cultural and Diversity Factors:

1. **Cultural Background:**
   - **Cultural Relevance:** Ensuring that media content is culturally relevant and sensitive to diverse audiences.

2. **Language Preferences:**
   - **Preferred Languages:** Analyzing language preferences for content consumption.

3. **Cultural Influences:**
   - **Impact of Culture on Preferences:** Understanding how cultural factors shape media consumption habits.

Audience Segmentation:

1. **Segmentation Analysis:**
   - **Creating Audience Segments:** Grouping the audience based on shared characteristics for targeted content delivery.

2. **User Personas:**
   - **Persona Development:** Creating fictional characters representing different segments to guide content creation.

Audience Feedback and Interaction:

1. **Surveys and Feedback:**
   - **Direct Audience Input:** Gathering feedback through surveys, polls, and direct interactions to understand preferences.

2. **Social Media Analytics:**

- **Monitoring Social Media:** Analyzing metrics like likes, shares, and comments for insights into audience engagement.

3. **User Reviews:**
   - **Review Analysis:** Examining user reviews and ratings for media content to gauge audience satisfaction.

Media audience analysis is an ongoing process that requires continuous monitoring and adaptation to changing audience dynamics. By gaining a deep understanding of their audience, media professionals can create content that resonates, attracts, and retains viewers, ultimately contributing to the success of media initiatives

Media Content Analysis

Media content analysis is a research method used to systematically analyze the content of media messages. It involves examining the characteristics, themes, patterns, and underlying meanings present in various forms of media content, such as text, images, audio, or video. Media content analysis is employed in various disciplines, including communication studies, journalism, sociology, and cultural studies. Here are key aspects of media content analysis:

Objectives of Media Content Analysis:

1. **Identifying Patterns and Themes:**
    - Analyzing media content to identify recurring patterns, themes, and messages.
2. **Understanding Representations:**
    - Examining how individuals, groups, and events are represented in media content.
3. **Detecting Biases and Stereotypes:**
    - Uncovering potential biases, stereotypes, or distorted portrayals within media messages.
4. **Assessing Tone and Emotion:**
    - Evaluating the emotional tone conveyed in media content and understanding how it may influence audiences.
5. **Measuring Frequency:**
    - Counting the frequency of specific elements or topics within media content.
6. **Exploring Framing:**
    - Analyzing how media frames and presents information, influencing audience perceptions.

Steps in Media Content Analysis:

1. **Define Research Questions:**
   - Clearly define the research questions or objectives guiding the content analysis.
2. **Select the Media Content:**
   - Choose the specific media content to be analyzed, whether it's newspaper articles, television programs, online articles, social media posts, or other forms of media.
3. **Develop Coding Categories:**
   - Create coding categories or variables that align with the research questions. Coding categories are labels or codes used to categorize elements within the content.
4. **Establish Coding Rules:**
   - Define coding rules to ensure consistency among coders. Specify how to identify and code relevant elements in the content.
5. **Train Coders:**
   - Train individuals (coders) who will be responsible for analyzing and coding the media content. Ensure they understand the coding categories and rules.
6. **Conduct the Content Analysis:**
   - Apply the coding categories to the selected media content. Systematically analyze and code each piece of content based on the established criteria.
7. **Interpret and Analyze Data:**
   - Analyze the coded data to conclude, identify patterns, and address the research questions. This may involve statistical analysis or qualitative interpretation.
8. **Report Findings:**
   - Present the findings of the content analysis in a clear

and organized manner. Communicate key patterns, themes, and insights derived from the analysis.

Types of Media Content Analysis:

1. **Manifest Content Analysis:**
    - Focuses on the visible, explicit elements in the media content, such as keywords, topics, or themes.
2. **Latent Content Analysis:**
    - Explores the underlying or hidden meanings, interpretations, or symbols present in media content.
3. **Quantitative Content Analysis:**
    - Involves numerical coding and statistical analysis to quantify the occurrence of specific elements or patterns in the content.
4. **Qualitative Content Analysis:**
    - Emphasizes the interpretation of content through a subjective analysis, often using coding to identify themes and meanings.
5. **Comparative Content Analysis:**
    - Compares media content across different sources, periods, or platforms to identify similarities or differences.

Challenges and Considerations:

1. **Inter-Coder Reliability:**
    - Ensuring consistency among coders to enhance the reliability of the content analysis.
2. **Sampling Issues:**
    - Addressing potential biases in the selection of media content for analysis.
3. **Contextual Understanding:**

- Recognizing the importance of understanding the broader context in which media content is produced and consumed.
4. **Ethical Considerations:**
    - Adhering to ethical guidelines, particularly when analyzing sensitive or controversial content.
5. **Dynamic Media Landscape:**
    - Acknowledging the dynamic nature of the media landscape and its impact on content analysis.

Media content analysis provides valuable insights into the construction of media messages, representations, and the influence of media on society. Researchers use this method to explore content across various media forms and to inform discussions about media influence, communication patterns, and cultural representations.

Surveys and Data Analysis

Surveys and data analysis are essential components of quantitative research, allowing researchers to collect and analyze information from a sample of individuals to conclude a larger population. Surveys are a popular method for gathering data, and once the data is collected, various statistical techniques can be applied for analysis. Here's an overview of surveys and the subsequent data analysis process:

Surveys:

1. **Definition:**
   - Surveys involve collecting information from individuals through a set of standardized questions. They can be conducted through interviews, questionnaires, or online forms.
2. **Types of Surveys:**
   - **Questionnaire Surveys:** Participants respond to a set of written or online questions.
   - **Interview Surveys:** Researchers ask questions verbally, often in a face-to-face or phone setting.
3. **Survey Design:**
   - **Question Construction:** Designing clear, unbiased questions to gather relevant information.
   - **Sampling:** Selecting a representative sample from the target population.
4. **Data Collection:**
   - Administering surveys to selected participants.
   - Ensuring reliability and validity of the survey instrument.
5. **Data Cleaning:**
   - Checking for errors or inconsistencies in the

collected data.
- Resolving any issues to ensure data quality.

Data Analysis:

1. **Descriptive Statistics:**
   - **Measures of Central Tendency:** Calculating mean, median, and mode.
   - **Measures of Dispersion:** Examining range, variance, and standard deviation.
2. **Frequency Distributions:**
   - Creating tables or charts to display the distribution of responses.
3. **Inferential Statistics:**
   - **Hypothesis Testing:** Assessing whether observed differences or relationships are statistically significant.
   - **Regression Analysis:** Examining the relationship between variables and predicting outcomes.
4. **Correlation Analysis:**
   - Assessing the strength and direction of relationships between variables.
5. **Chi-Square Analysis:**
   - Testing the independence of categorical variables.
6. **Cross-Tabulation:**
   - Examining relationships between two or more variables.
7. **Statistical Software:**
   - Using statistical software (e.g., SPSS, R, or Excel) to conduct analyses efficiently.
8. **Data Visualization:**
   - Creating charts, graphs, or other visual

representations to convey key findings.

9. **Reporting Results:**
    - Interpreting the results in the context of the research questions.
    - Presenting findings clearly and understandably.
10. **Statistical Significance:**
    - Determining whether observed effects are likely due to chance or are statistically significant.
11. **Margin of Error:**
    - Estimating the margin of error to understand the precision of survey results.
12. **Reliability and Validity:**
    - Assessing the reliability and validity of survey instruments and results.

Challenges and Considerations:

1. **Sampling Bias:**
    - Addressing potential biases introduced by the sampling process.
2. **Non-Response Bias:**
    - Accounting for bias introduced when participants choose not to respond.
3. **Question Wording:**
    - Ensuring clarity and neutrality in survey questions to avoid bias.
4. **Data Privacy:**
    - Protecting the privacy and confidentiality of participants.
5. **Response Rate:**
    - Managing low response rates and their potential impact on the generalizability of findings.
6. **Generalization:**

- Recognizing the limits of generalizing survey results to the broader population.

Applications:

1. **Market Research:**
    - Understanding consumer preferences and market trends.
2. **Public Opinion Research:**
    - Examining public attitudes and opinions on various issues.
3. **Social Science Research:**
    - Investigating social phenomena and behaviors.
4. **Health Research:**
    - Assessing health behaviors, outcomes, and perceptions.
5. **Employee Feedback:**
    - Gathering feedback from employees for organizational improvement.
6. **Education Research:**
    - Assessing student performance, satisfaction, and learning outcomes.

Surveys and data analysis are powerful tools for researchers, businesses, and policymakers to make informed decisions based on empirical evidence. Proper survey design, careful data collection, and robust statistical analysis are crucial for obtaining reliable and meaningful results.

Milton Keynes UK
Ingram Content Group UK Ltd.
UKHW020643220124
436466UK00019B/880